Amicus

The Studio That Made Us Scream and Scream Again

Thomas Baxter

Contents

INTRODUCTION

There was another British studio besides Hammer who did a fairly roaring trade in horror films in the sixties and seventies. Amicus (Latin for "friendship") Productions were created by Americans Milton Subotsky and Max J Rosenberg and - inspired by Hammer's fame - they gate-crashed the thriving (if thrifty) British horror scene. Rosenberg was a lawyer by trade while Subotsky was a horror and sci-fi buff who had worked as an editor in the army. At the time the British Government had an incentive that forced cinemas to show a quota of British made films and also offered tax breaks to British based productions. There was money to be made if you were shrewd enough and the Amicus legacy became a memorably enjoyable and colourful one.

The Eady Plan, which Amicus took advantage of, was a government scheme introduced in 1950 to support and promote British film production. It was named after Sir Wilfred Eady, who was a senior Treasury official at that time. Under the Eady Plan, a levy was imposed on cinema admissions, with a certain percentage of the ticket price being allocated to the British Film Production Fund. This fund was then used to finance the production and distribution of British films. The levy was compulsory and lasted from 1957 until 1985. Amicus also managed to attract enough private investors to remain largely independent.

Amicus were heavily influenced by the classic 1945 Ealing portmanteau chiller Dead of Night and although they produced all manner of films (from musical films to family Doctor Who adventures to espionage thrillers) they found their true niche with the anthology horror film. Four or five short tales within one film containing many famous guest stars - including crossover names from Hammer like Peter Cushing and Christopher Lee. Amicus would hire big name actors for a couple of days and that way star names could go on the poster without costing them too much money. So you'd get someone like Sir Ralph Richardson spending a day on Tales from the Crypt before going off to the West End at night to do a play.

Amicus also featured some young unknown actors too who went on to fame - like Michael Gambon, Charlotte Rampling and Donald Sutherland.

Amicus largely (but not always) eschewed the period and gothic trappings of Hammer and their anthology films were set in the present day. Because of this they remain a lot of fun now with the (obviously dated) seventies fashions. I actually have more vivid memories of watching the Amicus compendiums growing up than I do the Hammer films. Subotsky and Rosenberg based Amicus at Shepperton Studios. It was, in their words, a studio without walls and their business partnership was founded on a handshake rather than a contract. The relationship between them didn't always run smoothly but they had a knack of getting things done. They were very smart in managing to entice some big names (admittedly some of whom were on the way down) into their films and keeping costs minimal at the same time.

Amicus Productions was a small team who became like a family. Milton Subotsky shunned a fancy office in London and instead used a little wooden hut at Shepperton as his base of operations. The contemporary settings of the horror compendiums were not only a clever way to save money (by not having to recreate period settings with costumes and sets) but also helped to make their films distinct from most of the Hammer films. Subotsky was more of a writer while Rosenberg was the one with the head for business. It was generally Rosenberg who came up with the (sometimes lurid) titles and marketing strategies while Subotsky (whatever his limitations as a writer you couldn't fault his enthusiasm) was more concerned with screenplays and hiring interesting people.

The combined work ethic of the two men was formidable and even on their ramshackle budgets they made Amicus a real force in the industry for a time. Subotsky would sit in on the editing of the Amicus films to offer his suggestions. Rosenberg and Subotsky both read as many horror short stories and novels as they could in their search for stories that might be a good fit for an Amicus film. In the face of modern, more cutting edge American and Italian horror imports, the

British horror film of the type Amicus and Hammer were making was looking old-fashioned by the mid-seventies (and the deluge of anthology horror/mystery shows on television probably didn't help Amicus either given that anthology horror was their stock-in-trade). Subotsky once said, only half in jest perhaps, that he made horror films because - "... it was the only kind of cinema where you could avoid sex and violence."

It was true that the Amicus films were old fashioned (despite their contemporary trappings) but then that was all part of the charm. The films were distinctly British and happy to exist in their own little world. Amicus eventually branched off into some rather daft but colourful anachronistic family adventure sci-fi monster films that always seemed to have Doug McClure as the lead. They expired in the late seventies when Milton Subotsky and Max J Rosenberg went their separate ways. But what an enjoyable legacy they left behind for future generations to discover.

In the book that follows we will examine every film that Amicus made and offer what is hopefully an entertaining and affectionate overview of the legacy of this beloved studio.

In the concluding chapter we shall also look at the work Milton Subotsky and Max Rosenberg did after Amicus folded. So, open that decanter of brandy, make sure there aren't any voodoo dolls or disembodied hands lying around, stay out of those catacombs, lock the doors lest an escaped maniac dressed as Father Christmas be lurking, watch out for the Werewolf Break, and prepare to enter the spooky, mysterious, eclectic, and wonderful world of Amicus Productions!

IT'S TRAD, DAD! (1962)

Amicus weren't just responsible for anthology films in their relatively short (in studio terms) but hugely enjoyable years operating in cinema. Oh no. They produced a range of often weird and wonderful films. There were conventional horror films, family adventure films aimed at children, surreal espionage thrillers, eccentric sci-fi films, gothic thrillers, James Bondish spy films, even a drama and a vague attempt to make what you might call an exploitation film. They never had a huge amount of money to juggle with but Amicus were not afraid to take a few risks when the mood took them and they were always shrewd in spotting talented young actors - in addition to casting famous older names were happy to pick up some quick work as their careers wound down. The Amicus films are an eclectic bag and while not all of them are entirely successful it remains a great deal of fun to trawl through this back catalogue.

It's Trad, Dad! (aka Ring-A-Ding Rhythm) was the first film officially produced by Amicus Productions. It was directed by Richard Lester (who would become known for his film work with the Beatles and on the Superman franchise with Christopher Reeve) and written by Milton Subotsky. This is not a horror film but a light hearted musical film. Amicus made a couple of musical films in their first years after formation and then found their real niche with the horror genre and also family friendly sci-fi.

It appears that Amicus thought there might be money to be made in youth oriented musical films but then thought better of it quite sharpish and veered away from that. As such, the two musical films near the beginning of the Amicus story (a story we associate more than anything with horror) somewhat feel like out of place oddities which have stepped out of the lift on the wrong floor. Not to say these musicals are a complete waste of time though. They remain interesting time capsules of the early sixties and capture a specific period in British youth culture just prior to the guitar pop explosion of the sixties.

The premise of It's Trad, Dad! has a pair of teenagers

named Craig (Craig Douglas) and Helen (Helen Shapiro) fighting for the right to enjoy their love of jazz and music. The local mayor (Felix Felton), for reasons best known to himself, hates music and has banned the deployment of the jukebox and television in the coffee shop (old black and white British films are absolutely obsessed by coffee bars aren't they?) - or something along these lines. These are rather draconian powers for a humble mayor to wield! Suffice to say, the mayor is a right old grump and seems intent on stopping young people from having any fun whatsoever. Sounds slightly like the plot of Footloose doesn't it? Anyway, Craig and Helen decide to organise a big jazz concert to promote their passion for music. That'll show the stuffy old folks.

The flimsy plot of the film, such as it is, doesn't really matter and is just an excuse for It's Trad, Dad! to throw in as many musical guest stars as it can muster and - to its credit - it does manage to attract a lot of them. I gather though that copyright issues stopped many of them from performing the songs they were most associated with. Despite the linking plot (and narration by comic actor Deryck Guyler - he of Please Sir! and Sykes fame), It's Trad, Dad! is more like a concert film than a conventional film. The actual concert never feels like it is part of the same film as the nonsense about banning the jukebox. This threadbare linking device always veers on the edge of feeling slightly pointless. Once a music numbers kick in it feels more like watching a very old edition of Top of the Pops and you forget that there even is a plot.

One of the main leads here is Helen Shapiro. Shapiro was a famous singer in Britain at the time. In 1961, Shapiro had two British number ones with You Don't Know and Walkin' Back to Happiness. Here's the remarkable thing though. Shapiro was a schoolgirl when she became a star. She was only fifteen when It's Trad, Dad! came out. Shapiro actually left school at fourteen to become a singer (which I'm pretty sure you wouldn't be allowed to do today). If they made this film nowadays, the Shapiro part would probably be played by some twenty-eight year-old model pretending to be a teenager. It's quite novel to see a 'youth' film where the teenagers are relatively normal and still kids in real life too.

Shapiro is a very likeable presence in the film and has a down to earthness that is rather charming. She feels like someone who could live next door or work in the local chip shop. Shapiro is no great shakes as an actor but it feels like she is just playing herself in the film so it doesn't really matter too much. She belts out several songs in the film in fine fashion. It's Trad, Dad! captures her at the high water mark of her short brush with fame. Once pop music and guitars came in and you had a new wave of female singers like Sandie Shaw *, Helen Shapiro suddenly seemed old hat at the tender age of sixteen. I gather that when Shapiro went out of fashion she took to the working clubs and carried on singing. She can always say though that she once topped the bill when she appeared with The Beatles in their early days.

Amicus were shrewd enough to throw in a number of American acts here to boost the international appeal of the film. The American artists shot their contributions in the United States and then were spliced into the film (you can tell too because you don't see the British audience during these numbers). There are a vast slew of musical guest stars in the film and the musical numbers are pleasant enough and distinct from the vague plot that loosely connects everything together. The plot of the film doesn't really matter. You get Gene Vincent, Chubby Checker, The Paris Sisters, and many others.

Shapiro's main co-star is Craig Douglas, who was also a popular singer in Britain at the time. Like Shapiro though, his time at the top was short lived. He had his last hit in 1963 and ended up singing on cruise ships. He can though, like Shapiro, say that he once topped a bill which included The Beatles. The actual staging of the concert scenes isn't what you'd describe as slick but Richard Lester does manage to bring a choppy energy to proceedings which helps the film survive some of the jazzy interludes. Only two years later he would direct A Hard Day's Night. You could say then that It's Trad, Dad! was sort of like his film school and helped him cut his teeth on this type of film.

There are a number of familiar faces in It's Trad, Dad! besides the musical guest stars. Alan 'Fluff' Freeman makes an appearance (I wonder if this was how Fluff got his part in Dr Terror's House of Horrors? Presumably, Milton Subotsky and Freeman became friends on this film?) and understandably seems more at home in this concert film musical world than he did in Dr Terror's House of Horrors. He is drawn into the film because the teenagers seek out disc jockeys to help them. The cockney comic actor Arthur Mullard (later to appear in Vault of Horror) also features, as do presenters/disc jockeys David Jacobs and Pete Murray. It's Trad, Dad! is unavoidably dated and a few of the musical acts might have you glancing at your watch but - generally - this is an interesting musical film that will probably appeal more to those who like the music from this era. Trivia - Milton Subotsky said that It's Trad, Dad! was his favourite film out of the ones he worked on. I suppose he must have liked musical films.

* Sandie Shaw shot to fame in the 1960s armed with a supernatural voice, equally supernatural cheekbones, and a Vidal Sassoon bob. She had eight top ten singles and three number ones (she was only a teenager when she had her first one with the Burt Bacharach/Hal David song There's Always Something There to Remind Me) and was the first entrant from the United Kingdom to win the Eurovision Song Contest with Puppet on a String. Sandie Shaw fans tend to gloss over this particular song though and she hated it too (although I believe she has mellowed somewhat on her Eurovision experience in recent years). Despite her fame and vaguely exotic looks there always seemed to be something ordinary about Sandie Shaw that was very appealing. She was born in Dagenham and worked in a factory for a while and you could probably imagine her leaving an arena after a show and getting a bag of chips on the way home. You could picture Sandie Shaw drinking tea in a cafe with a sticky bun just as easily as you could imagine her at some swanky party.

JUST FOR FUN (1963)

Just for Fun was directed by Gordon Flemyng and written by Milton Sobotsky. Flemyng would later direct the two Doctor Who films that Amicus made. In his last years he directed on television shows like Minder and Lovejoy. Just for Fun is another early musical film from Amicus. Milton Subotsky said this film was hobbled because - unlike the first film - it wasn't made with EMI. Subotsky said EMI had all the hip and 'cool' new music artists in 1963 - none of which could appear in Just For Fun!

The linking device here makes even less sense than it did with It's Trad, Dad! and isn't really an important part of the film. They just need an excuse for all the musical numbers to occur. The premise has the Prime Minister (Richard Vernon) angling for the youth vote but (stupidly) cutting the amount of pop music on television. That's clearly not a manifesto pledge designed to appeal to music mad youngsters in the 1960s. As a consequence, teenagers decide to reject the political parties and form their own one. To this end, they draft in a number of pop singers to help them. And so, once again, another thinly veiled concert film transpires.

This is a decent enough musical film although the names on offer here seem somewhat less stellar than they were in It's Trad, Dad! on the whole. Brian Poole and the Tremeloes, Joe Brown, Bobby Vee, and so on. There'll be a large number of acts in the film you've never heard of. I don't think you'll be missing any pivotal moments in music history if you never get around to sitting through the whole of Just for Fun. It's all quite well done though for the time and the eclectic nature of the film manages to navigate it through some lulls.

There are a lot comedy vignettes around the music and although none of these are very funny they do at least give the film a madcap energy at times. As with It's Trad, Dad!, it isn't so much that this is a very good film (because it isn't really) but more the fact that it serves as an interesting little time capsule on what was considered to be 'hip' in the Britain of 1963. It's Trad, Dad! made a tidy little profit for Amicus but

Just for Fun didn't do so well and is generally regarded to be a weaker film. After this film came out Amicus evidently decided to move away from these types of 'Britpop' films and do something else entirely.

Unavoidably, there are going to be musical numbers here that you could happily live without but some of them are very good and even anticipate the pop music that would dominate in the sixties. Interestingly, the camera operator for the film was Nicholas Roeg. Roeg makes Just for Fun look like a primitive form of music television before there was such a thing as music television. There's not really the anarchic spirit here you get with some sixties concert/music films but Roeg is doing his best to put his own little stamp on the film and it's always competent enough with a few nice little flourishes here and there.

The background extras in old films like this are always fun and quite amusing from a modern perspective. You get lots of young women with beehive hairstyles and some spotty young men with jumpers and ties on. They all gyrate away in preposterous fashion. Pop star of the era Mark Wynter is the main lead and he's alright if a trifle bland. Billy Fury he is not. Wynter had a bit more staying power than Craig Douglas and was a star for most of the sixties. He was also a stage actor and so he's a bit more competent in the thesping department than your average singer turned actor - if still not exactly Laurence Olivier. Wynter was later in the British horror film The Haunted House of Horror (a comic haunted house caper with Frankie Avalon and a young Richard O'Sullivan) in 1969.

Sadly, there is no Helen Shapiro this time around though. It's a shame they couldn't have got Shapiro back and made this more of a direct sequel of sorts. Perhaps the fifteen minutes of fame afforded to Helen Shapiro was nearly up by the time they made this. Just for Fun is, like It's Trad, Dad!, awash with familiar faces away from the musical acts. Alan Freeman (who seems to be enjoying himself again and in his element in this world of music and teeny boppers) and David Jacobs return to play disc jockeys (I suppose they are really just playing themselves). Unfortunately, Jimmy Savile also features as one of the disc jockeys in Just for Fun. Amicus could hardly know what the future held but it obviously doesn't add too much in the way of charm and enjoyment to an old film these days when you see Jimmy Savile in the cast. Presumably, they'd edit Savile out now if they showed this on television.

Other familiar faces in Just for Fun include Kenny Lynch (who would of course return to Amicus for Dr Terror's House of Horrors), Irene Handl, and Dick Emery (Dick Emery was a very famous comedian in the seventies who played many sorts of characters in his sketch shows, sort of like the Harry Enfield of his day you might say). Just for Fun feels a slight step down from It's Trad, Dad! with the slightly less famous names and the lack of Helen Shapiro but if you did like the previous Amicus musical film you'll probably get some enjoyment out of this one too. Just for Fun is rather silly in its linking premise and unavoidably dated but it serves as another time capsule window into this specific period of British cinema and music. From here on in though it would be, with one or two exceptions, horror and sci-fi for Amicus.

DR TERROR'S HOUSE OF HORRORS (1965)

Dr Terror's House of Horrors was directed by Freddie Francis and kick-started the Amicus series of British compendium horror films. The film was shot at Shepperton Studios with a budget of £105,000. Amicus creative chiefs Milton Subotsky and Max J Rosenberg decided to take on rival Hammer (Subotsky had apparently submitted a Frankenstein script to Hammer before their success with the old Universal staples but the script was rejected and left him with a certain bitterness towards the famed horror studio *) by adopting the anthology structure of the classic 1945 Ealing film Dead of Night (the treatment for Dr Terror's House of Horrors apparently dated way back to the era just after Dead of Night).

Dr Terror's House of Horrors is the real start of the Amicus story because the horror anthology would become their stock-in-trade. It is the horror anthologies that Amicus are most famous for and the horror anthologies that we love the most in their catalogue. I rewatch the Amicus anthology films every year and I never get tired of them. There is just something wonderfully entertaining and cosy about them. Anthology horror films were certainly not a new idea - even in 1965. Anthology horror films have been a staple of the genre for at least a hundred years. Richard Oswald's Eerie Tales (Unheimliche Geschichten) was released way back in 1919 and offered stories by Poe and Robert Louis Stevenson framed by paintings in a supernatural bookshop.

The structure of the anthology film is usually the same. You get a number of stories (modern anthology horror films seem to have an awful lot while the old anthologies were usually more compact with three or four) and a framing device/wraparound of some sort to link the tales. The framing device of the horror anthology film is usually great fun. I'm always disappointed when I encounter a horror anthology that eschews this tradition and plunges us straight into the opening story.

The Citizen Kane of anthology horror films is Ealing's 1945 portmanteau chiller Dead of Night. This film is so good it still provides a few shivers today all these years later. Dead of Night was the touchstone and the inspiration. The 1960s and 1970s were the boom decades for the anthology horror film. It was in these decades that Amicus made their famous compendium horrors in Britain and - elsewhere - we had classics like Kwaidan in Japan and Black Sabbath in Italy. Vincent Price also starred in the enjoyably colourful Twice-Told Tales and Tales of Terror.

Amicus latching onto the anthology film was shrewd in hindsight because it distinguished them from Hammer. They were good at making anthology films too. By way of example, look at the other British anthology horror films made in or around the Amicus era - like Tales That Witness Madness, The Uncanny, and The Monster Club (and Milton Subotsky had a hand in those last two films - as we'll discuss later). While these films have their moments there is something a bit off about them. They don't have the cosy charm and entertainment factor of the Amicus films. Horror purists can be a trifle sniffy about the Amicus anthology horror films but to be nitpicky about them is to completely miss the point. These films are pure fun and great at what they do. The only one for me that doesn't quite live up to this blueprint is Torture Garden - but we'll get to that soon enough.

A number of Hammer veterans were signed for Dr Terror's House of Horrors - not least genre icons Peter Cushing and Christopher Lee but also the director Freddie Francis (also of course an award winning cinematographer) and composer Elisabeth Lutyens. Lutyens was the first woman to score a horror film and enjoyed her status as the "Queen of horror".

Donald Sutherland, later to become a star through films like M*A*S*H, Kelly's Heroes and Don't Look Now, was an unknown Canadian actor based in Britain at the time. He had studied at the London Academy of Music and Dramatic Art and spent a year and a half in Repertory Theatre in Scotland. Dr Terror's House of Horrors was one of his early roles. Sutherland got $5,400 for the film and a free ride to work every morning with Max Rosenberg.

Christopher Lee had an incredible 250+ screen credits to his name when he died. Lee was born in Westminster in 1922, the son of a Boer War veteran and Italian contessa. During World War 2 he was an intelligence officer in the Long Range Desert Patrol missions which formed the basis of the SAS. He had actually volunteered for the 1939/40 Finnish "Winter War" (when the Soviet Union invaded Finland and despite outnumbering the Fins in terms of soldiers, tanks and aircraft to a preposterous degree had a nightmarishly difficult campaign) prior to North Africa. He was also an RAF pilot until an eye injury grounded him. You honestly couldn't make up Lee's life if you tried. James Bond and Indiana Jones had nothing on him.

The North African campaign defeated the Africa Korps made famous by Rommel and - crucially - stopped the Middle Eastern and Persian oil fields from falling into Axis hands. It also laid the foundation for the Allied invasion of Italy. Lee took part in this campaign too and climbed Mount Vesuvius three days before it erupted. He was at the Battle of Monte

Cassino and also served in Churchill's Special Operations Executive - an elite organisation involved in espionage, sabotage and reconnaissance in Nazi dominated Europe. The unofficial name for the SOE was The Ministry of Ungentlemanly Warfare.

The SOE's activities are still classified and so Lee would never speak about his time serving with them. When the war ended, the multi-lingual Lee hunted Nazis for the Central Registry of War Criminals and Security Suspects before turning his hand to acting at the age of 25. He had the first of his many film credits in 1948's Corridor of Mirrors (directed by Terence Young) and his path would eventually lead to Hammer Studios and his iconic portrayal of Dracula. Because Lee was such a commanding (6'5 in height) and polished presence it only took some contact lenses, a cape and a bit of make-up magic to turn him into a memorable Prince of Darkness. Lee and his great friend Peter Cushing were wonderful at lending class and gravitas to these old horror films.

The actor, musician, and later beloved children's entertainer/presenter Roy Castle was added to Dr Terror's House of Horrors as jazz trumpeter "Biff" Bailey after Acker Bilk had to bail out due to ill health. The strangest cast member is surely Alan "Fluff" Freeman - who famously inspired the Harry Enfield character Dave Nice. The disc jockey and Top of the Pops presenter plays Bill Rogers in the "killer plant" segment of the film. Freeman was tentatively exploring an acting career at the time but his wooden performance in Dr Terror's House of Horrors seemed to put an end to this ambition. It seems that Fluff very wisely decided to stick to the day job after giving the old acting racket an experimental whirl. He had short roles in three more films - sensibly playing disc jockeys in two of them. Freeman also had a cameo in the musical film Absolute Beginners.

Dr Terror's House of Horrors took around five weeks to shoot and wrapped on the 3rd of July 1964. It was released on the 5th of February 1965. The stories in the film were apparently based on decades old spooky yarns that Milton Subotsky had written for American radio. The film begins with a group of men (played by Alan Freeman, Neil McCallum, Donald Sutherland, Roy Castle, and Christopher Lee respectively) boarding a railway carriage on a fog billowed platform and sitting down in one of the compartments. There isn't much room left but, just before the train departs, one more traveller - the mysterious Doctor Schreck played by the great Peter Cushing - wants to get in.

Once in the compartment with the men, Schreck soon snoozes off to sleep and his deck of Tarot cards spills out. "That's a funny looking deck man," says Roy Castle helpfully. Schreck, a "Doctor of Metaphysics", duly offers to use the cards to predict the future of each man, much to the annoyance in particular of Christopher Lee as sceptical and snooty art critic Franklyn Marsh. Marsh thinks that Schreck is nothing more than a charlatan. A confidence trickster. But he will he be proved right about this? Well, given that this is an Amicus anthology horror film, I certainly wouldn't rush out to place any bets on that at the bookies.

The framing device - always of course an important component of the anthology film - works well enough in Dr Terror's House of Horrors for a number of reasons. First of all, the night train carriage location is atmospheric and could be conveyed in an effective fashion without requiring elaborate sets or special effects (Amicus never had the most lavish budgets at their disposal). Secondly, the framing device also brings all the main characters in the film together in a confined space, most saliently of course Peter Cushing and Christopher Lee. Why is this important? Well, because we want to see Cushing and Lee together onscreen if we can! We do and their sparring as the mysterious Schreck and the irritated and pompous Marsh is always enjoyable.

The first story is called Werewolf and features Neil McCallum (like Donald Sutherland, McCallum was a Canadian based in Britain at the time) as Jamie Dawson, an architect who travels back to his old home in the Scottish Highlands to make some alterations for the new owner. There is however something not quite right about his old family home with strange noises soon coming from something prowling outside and the disappearance of the key to the cellar. Do spooky butler/groundskeeper Caleb (Peter Madden) and maid Valda (Katy Wild) know more than they are letting on? When Jamie does manage to investigate the cellar he finds a wall with fresh plaster concealing a dusty coffin. Could this be the resting place of Cosmo Valdemar, a former owner of the house who swore a curse on those that followed?

A fairly solid first story, Werewolf, like Dr Terror's House of Horrors as a whole, is quite patently studio bound and restrictive in scope but still works relatively well with spooky stairways and cobwebbed cellars shrouded in half-light. The anachronistic aura (Scotland is depicted as being like something from Medieval times!) is both ludicrous and enjoyable at the same time and while there obviously wasn't an awful lot of money to spare in the production of this story they make the best of what they have and manage to generate some sense of atmosphere.

McCallum's Scottish accent isn't bad although you would probably have to be Scottish to have the definitive say on this! He makes Jamie Dawson suitably wide-eyed as the strange goings on escalate and Peter Madden makes a nice enigmatic (and possibly mad) butler. Neil McCallum later appeared in television shows like UFO and Jason King but sadly died in 1976 when he was only 46. This story has quite a good almost Gothic ambiance and is the one segment here that possibly could have been stretched out into a longer mystery or even made a decent little low-budget feature length film in its own right. In many ways it's one of the more atypical Amicus compendium segments with its vague sense of time and period.

You'll probably spot the ending a mile off but this is good fun nonetheless and certainly quite gripping at times as Dawson investigates the cellar and makes some eerie discoveries. Werewolf perhaps lacks the overblown style and arch melodrama of the American Poe/Vincent Price anthology film stories of the era but it serves as a competent introduction to the Amicus compendium franchise. What helps Dr Terror's House of Horrors is that the performances by the actors are played reasonably straight - however fantastical the situations are. Bernard Lee seems a bit bored in The Creeping Vine and

Michael Gough is a trifle arch in Disembodied Hand but most of the performances in the film are fairly earnest.

The next segment is The Creeping Vine and stars (for reasons probably best known to the producers of the film) legendary DJ Alan Freeman as Bill Rogers. Bill returns from a holiday with his wife Ann (Ann Bell) and daughter Carrole (Phoebe Sarah Nicholls) only to find a strange, leafy vine has taken root in the garden and wrapped itself around part of the house. I quite like a wild overgrown garden myself but Bill is determined to get rid of the vine. The vine, which seems to move of its own accord, refuses to yield to garden shears and eventually takes a disliking to the family dog. A perplexed Bill turns to professors Drake and Hopkins, played by Jeremy Kemp and Bernard Lee respectively. This pesky plant is soon proving to be very dangerous indeed.

The Creeping Vine is a rather silly (although to be fair no one in the cast seems to be taking this nonsense too seriously) but oddly enjoyable second segment for Dr Terror's House of Horrors. A genial Freeman (perhaps wondering what on earth he is doing in the film in the first place) smiles throughout practically the entire story whatever perils the killer plant is threatening. No matter what happens, Freeman's facial expression rarely changes. Given that actors generally tend to convey fluctuating emotions through their face, well, you can see why old Fluff didn't have much of an acting career.

Freeman's performance might not be the stuff of Oscar acceptance speeches but his presence does in a strange way make Dr Terror's House of Horrors more curious and cultish. It is undeniably a unique experience to watch Freeman and Bernard Lee (who was of course M in the James Bond films) trapped in a house by an intelligent, indestructible plant. Only someone with the authority of Bernard Lee could get away with lines like "A plant like that could take over the world!" Let's be honest, it's hard to believe that the unruly vine (which moves incredibly slowly) in Freeman's back garden is ever going to take over the world! That vine would be hard pressed to get to the end of the street.

Ann Bell, who play's Bill's wife in The Creeping Vine, would go to be in virtually every television show ever made. The Bill,

Holby City, Inspector Morse, and so on. She is probably best known though for playing Marion in the war drama Tenko. Phoebe Sarah Nicholls, who plays the little girl in this segment, later played John Merrick's mother in the David Lynch film The Elephant Man. Phoebe Sarah Nicholls has enjoyed a long and busy acting career since Dr Terror's House of Horrors. She's been in everything from Brideshead Revisited to I'm Alan Partridge to Transformers: The Last Knight.

The Creeping Vine is not exactly Day of the Triffids (a film version of which was co-directed by Freddie Francis) and never really goes anywhere but the pure brazen daftness of this story is entertaining enough although - and this is perhaps a general criticism of Dr Terror's House of Horrors as a whole - it could have been a tad scarier with a couple of twists. If one had to be pedantic you could say that this segment never really develops much in the duration of its (admittedly shortish) running time. Still, if you can't at least glean some enjoyment from a segment where an intelligent plant cuts phone lines and traps Fluff Freeman and James Bond's boss in a house then there is really no hope for you.

Next up to have his fortune told by Doctor Schreck is jazz musician Biff Bailey - played by Roy Castle - in the segment called Voodoo. Voodoo is the only segment in the film that makes any attempt to go for a Swinging Sixties backdrop with its jazz musicians and nightclub scenes. Biff and his chirpy cockney band, as Doctor Schreck predicts, are naturally delighted when told they are headed to exotic Haiti for a tour. But once there, Biff just can't resist nosing around and pilfering the local voodoo beat in the form of some scribbled notes - despite expressly being warned not to. "Do not steal from the god Dambala!" Back in England, what will happen when Biff and his group attempt to play these forbidden voodoo tunes? Something supernatural I'd wager.

This is quite a fun segment and it really wouldn't be an Amicus anthology film with at least one hokey voodoo themed story. Although the tone here is more humorous than anything (and it does contain a calypso musical number by Kenny Lynch that we probably could have happily lived without) this story does have a few creepy and atmospheric moments - especially back in London where Castle is spooked walking down some dark streets at night with the wind picking up and litter fluttering on the breeze. Haiti is obviously not a location shoot but a few Carry On Up the Jungle style sets but it's all part of the ramshackle charm.

Voodoo is hopelessly dated but then it was made a long time ago and these sorts of films are not to be taken too seriously. You couldn't get away today with the general 'don't trust foreigners, they are all highly mysterious and primitive and probably into black magic or something' air that permeates this story. Roy Castle, a much more competent actor than the hapless Alan Freeman was in the last segment, is good value as Biff and throws himself into the part with his customary enthusiasm. He does make Biff believably terrified at times and although he did something he shouldn't have done we root for Biff all the same because it is impossible not to like Roy Castle.

It helps too of course that Roy Castle can play his trumpet for real and so makes the musical sequences more convincing. Perhaps the biggest criticism one could have with Voodoo is that the ending feels a bit weak and sudden and so makes the segment as a whole feel more underwhelming than it should have been. One flaw with Dr Terror's House of Horrors is that it doesn't give the audience any outrageous twists. You can predict fairly accurately the how the various denouements will pan out. Voodoo is very silly at times but it does have some atmospheric flourishes and the musical interludes are not with their charms. You wouldn't say this was the best segment in Dr Terror's House of Horrors but it is entertaining and a fairly breezy segment that doesn't outstay its welcome.

The best story, Disembodied Hand, is next and features Christopher Lee as the pompous and vitriolic art critic Franklyn Marsh - a man who makes Brian Sewell look like Frank Spencer. "Very well. Shuffle your cards, foretell my destiny," snorts the sceptical Marsh to Doctor Schreck in the train compartment. We then see Marsh in an art gallery mercilessly trashing the work of painter Eric Landor (Michael Gough) with enormous glee and pomposity as a group of sycophants hang onto his every word.

Marsh is a celebrity critic who has made himself famous for his rants against modern art, with Landor a particular target. Landor gains his revenge by having a new piece of work brought out for Marsh to evaluate. "This is highly irregular," snaps Marsh but eventually agrees. "Now this is quite a different matter," he says when he looks at the work, praising it as wildly as he trashed Landor's work. An amused Landor reveals the artist was a chimpanzee (!) and Marsh is suitably humiliated. Landor then follows Marsh around to public engagements constantly reminding him of his chimp themed goof and generally begins to ruin his career. How can Marsh salvage his career and reputation? Well, no prizes for guessing that one. He's soon plotting to get rid of Landor for good.

Disembodied Hand gains a big boost from some good acting by Christopher Lee, who is gloriously snotty and panto villain posh as Marsh, and Michael Gough, who elicits genuine sympathy from the audience at times. While this segment is as daft as they come ultimately (with disembodied rubber hand shenanigans) it is always tremendous fun to be in the company of Christopher Lee as things go from bad to worse for Marsh and his confident and crisp urbane air begins to slip into panic and uncertainty. Like The Creeping Vine, this segment slides into 'so ludicrous it's funny territory' but it is enjoyable and the presence of Lee and Michael Gough lends some gravitas to the hokey proceedings.

Franklyn Marsh makes a great Amicus villain too because not only is he insufferably arrogant, his essential stock-in-trade is trashing the hard work of other people and when he is made to look somewhat foolish his response is to resort to murder! We enjoy watching him taken down a peg or two (or three even) during the course of the story. What of the severed hand capers? Well, this is of course the sort of horror staple that is hard to do with appearing silly or unintentionally amusing but we must remember that this is an Amicus anthology film not the collected works of Ingmar Bergman. Some hokiness is a part of the charm is it not?

The last future to be told is that of Bob Carroll (played by a very young Donald Sutherland) in a segment called Vampire.

Bob and his French wife Nicolle (Jennifer Jayne) move to a small New England town where Bob is to become a local doctor but their arrival seems to coincide with a strange outbreak of "pernicious anemia", or, in other words; someone or something is draining blood from the local population. Strange cases start to pop up in Bob's surgery of fang marks and colleague Dr Blake (Max Adrian) comments that "If this were Medieval times I'd almost say he was a victim of a vampire!" However, Bob is not laughing when Blake points the finger of suspicion at his wife Nicolle. Can she really be a vampire?

A rather enjoyable and fairly playful vampire mystery to end the stories in Dr Terror's House of Horrors, Vampire does benefit from a twist ending (albeit a predictable one) of sorts and a pleasant sense of atmosphere. We never actually believe that they've ventured abroad to depict anywhere in America but we go with the ambiance. It's agreeable fun when Bob and Blake turn detective to try and see if Nicolle is really a vampire and as each story in Dr Terror's House of Horrors is only about fifteen minutes or so it doesn't outstay its welcome either.

That is obviously one of the strengths of the anthology structure. If you don't like a particular segment it doesn't matter too much because another one will be along soon. Sutherland is very watchable in this early role although British actress Jennifer Jayne is possibly not the most convincing French accented person ever put on film. They make a nice couple though. Max Adrian, an Irish actor and veteran of stage and screen, seems to be enjoying his supporting role as Dr Blake. The only glaring weaknesses of Vampire are - as we have mentioned - the fact that you might spot the twist coming and it never really convinces you that the characters are in the United States in a small town. Obviously, they weren't really. They were probably freezing to death in some draughty and modest set at Shepperton!

We then of course return to the railway carriage where the train journey is coming to an end and Doctor Schreck is about to reveal to these men their true fates and his ultimate identity. If you've seen subsequent Amicus compendium horror films then the ending will come as no surprise whatsoever but I always enjoy the linking device and final predictable fate of the characters in these films and the framing scene in this film works well enough with Cushing, Lee and the rest in the railway carriage. In particular, the banter between the sceptical, snooty Lee and the enigmatic Cushing is wonderful.

Dr Terror's House Of Horrors is a lot of fun although, obviously, it has dated somewhat. The film is very low budget and studio bound which sometimes makes it seem restricted but isn't a major drawback overall, often adding to the charm of the piece. It still looks quite good too with some nice use of Techniscope colour by Freddie Francis. Perhaps the tone is a tad too humorous at times here and the film could probably have done with a few more scares and twists in the tale but if you have a fondness for these old anthology pictures you'll have a good time, not least for the famous (and slightly eccentric) cast and the opportunity to see horror legends Christopher Lee and Peter Cushing onscreen together. Dr Terror's House Of Horrors serves as a firm foundation for the Amicus anthology film and several more would soon be on the way.

* The Curse of Frankenstein is a 1957 Hammer film, loosely based on the 1818 novella Frankenstein by Mary Shelley. It was Hammer's first colour horror film and the first of their (many) Frankenstein pictures. The film was directed by Terence Fisher and written by Jimmy Sangster. It was apparently Max Rosenberg who came to Hammer with the idea of doing a Frankenstein film and he even gave them a script by Milton Subotsky. Rosenberg claimed that Hammer stiffed him out of a profit share deal for this film and just gave him a modest flat fee. This, presumably, is perhaps what motivated Rosenberg and Subotsky to set up Amicus - who became Hammer's main British horror rival. If this story is true you could say that Amicus Productions was, to use a Curb Your Enthusiasm reference, a spite store!

DR WHO AND THE DALEKS (1965)

Dr Who and the Daleks was directed by Gordon Flemyng and written by Milton Subotsky (it is said though that David Whitaker really wrote the film on the instruction of Terry Nation - Nation allowing Subotsky to have the screen credit as along as Whitaker was brought in as a writer). The film is loosely based on the 1963 television stories The Dead Planet and The Daleks. The Daleks has the first Doctor - in the guise of William Hartnell - meeting his eternal intergalactic foes the Daleks and people hid behind sofas everywhere as these metal encased baddies entered the pantheon of television history. The Daleks, sinister aliens in metal transporters forever bent on universal conquest, were a wondrous Terry Nation creation and terrified generations of children. There would be scarier Doctor Who episodes but nothing would quite have the impact of the Daleks meeting us for the first time. Terry Nation sat in on a few production meetings for Dr Who and the Daleks but evidently didn't want to write the film himself.

Dr Who and the Daleks was the first of two films Amicus made based on the famous BBC television show. Amicus bought an option from the BBC to make two Doctor Who films for the modest sum of £500. I bet you couldn't do that today! One slightly odd thing is that the two Amicus Doctor Who films still remain the only two big screen adventures for this iconic character. For some reason no one has since made a Doctor Who feature film for cinemas - which is strange when you think about it. In the 1970s literally everything on British television got a big screen spin-off film - from On the Buses to Doomwatch to The Sweeney to For the Love of Ada. But there was no new Doctor Who film. Imagine a Doctor Who film in the late 1970s with a budget, good special effects, and Tom Baker. That would have been great wouldn't it?

Amicus released Dr Who and the Daleks under the newly created AARU production banner in order to separate this family film from their usual (and soon to be far more frequent) horror fare. Another salient reason for this is that the financier Joe Vegoda owned AARU and had been instrumental in helping to fund the production budget of Dr Who and the Daleks. In return for putting his hands in his pockets, Vegoda wanted his company to get some promotion through the film. As far as the actual production went though this was still very much an Amicus film.

The main motivation of Amicus for buying the rights to Dr Who was the 'Dalekmania' sweeping Britain at the time. People just couldn't get enough of the Daleks. The decision by Amicus to make these films was a shrewd one as they were very popular in the domestic (British) box-office market and children in particular loved them. As for adults and Doctor Who fans, well, they tend to be a lot more lukewarm about this film. Dr Who and the Daleks, nostalgia aside, doesn't have an especially good reputation and is aimed squarely at a young audience.

Dr Who and the Daleks is not considered to be part of the Doctor Who canon or history but just its own thing completely separate from the BBC's version of Doctor Who on television. In this film, the Doctor is not an alien Time Lord from the planet Gallifrey but an eccentric human inventor. I gather though that at the time this was actually in line with the television show because all the lore about Gallifrey and Time Lords had yet to be established. William Hartnell was not asked to reprise his television role as the Doctor for this film (which apparently annoyed Hartnell because he would have loved to do a Doctor Who film) and so the Doctor is instead played by Amicus favourite Peter Cushing. It appears that Amicus decided that William Hartnell wasn't well known outside of Britain and wanted a more famous actor to play the Doctor.

Cushing, in a performance that was not to all tastes, deploys his rather comic 'doddery old man' routine for the part. It was the sort of performance he would later use again in the Amicus film At the Earth's Core. Peter Cushing's version of the Doctor is a bumbling sweet grandfather who is smart but sort of clumsy. The Doctor in the story is a professor and inventor on Earth who has invented an incredible machine called the

TARDIS which can travel through space and time. Terry Nation later expressed what you might call a lack of enthusiasm for Cushing's Doctor and the film in general. "He was a little too gentle... too kindly and too warm. The thing that Bill (Hartnell) had was this irascibility... he was a bad tempered, old, curmudgeonly figure... I'd like to have seen more of that in the character."

To be fair to Peter Cushing he did say the following regarding the two Dr Who films - "They were very enjoyable. A little frustrating, though, because they were not quite what we planned. I think I speak for everyone involved when I say that we intended to make them a little darker. But they turned out well, very good entertainments and a hit with the children." When it came to the crunch, Amicus were more interested in making a film that might appeal to kids rather than making a film that might impress Terry Nation. While this meant the film would have limited appeal for Doctor Who purists going forward, it was a sensible business decision at time because Dr Who and the Daleks was one of the top twenty films at the British box-office in 1965. Interestingly, Cushing later admitted he had turned down an offer to play the Doctor in the BBC television series twice in the 1960s because he wanted to make films rather than work on the small screen.

What is the plot of Dr Who and the Daleks? An accident propels the Doctor, his granddaughters Susan (Roberta Tovey), Barbara (Jennie Linden), and Barbara's boyfriend Ian (Roy Castle), through time and space in the TARDIS to a dying planet where a city is occupied by those metal encased intergalactic villains the Daleks. The Daleks are intent on wiping out a race of humans known as the Thals and - needless to say - the Doctor and his friends become embroiled in all the drama and danger.

Dr Who and the Daleks is a film that fans of the television show sometimes tend to be a little on the sniffy side about whenever it rears its head in conversation. This is mostly because it is not canon and so therefore can never be a true part of the history of the character. It would be fun to see the television show do an episode where they somehow made Cushing's Doctor canon! Maybe he lost his memory and thought he was human? Perhaps the other reason for the sniffiness is the fact that Dr Who and the Daleks is unashamedly a film for children. The television show is also aimed at children but it has references, jokes, and horror elements that give it a broader appeal too. The television show is frequently much darker and more melodramatic than the Amicus films based on this iconic property. Dr Who and the Daleks is much more family friendly and undemanding than the television source.

Dr Who and the Daleks is very much of a product of its time with the jazzy sixties atmosphere (the Thals look like beatniks with their pudding bowl haircuts and waistcoats) and Cushing's rather avuncular doddery grandfather Doctor a long way removed from the character we've seen in the television show over the decades. If you aren't too obsessed though about the continuity of Doctor Who or expecting 2001: A Space Odyssey, then Dr Who and the Daleks is actually quite good fun. The eye popping colour of the film is enjoyable (especially from a modern vantage point where films often look dark and grainy) and there are some decent sets and designs too. Doctor Who in its early television years and decades was a famously bargain basement production so it's fun to contrast that with the scope and colour that Dr Who and the Daleks throws at the screen.

I would imagine that kids used to the black and white television show on a tiny television were very impressed by this colourful widescreen transplant of the character in this film. An obvious problem though is that the spooky 'behind the sofa' atmosphere generated in the black and white television show is completely lost in this bright and spangly film. The Daleks are not very menacing or scary in this film at all (which is a shame) and they are also required to deliver far too much exposition at times. The Daleks appearing to be armed with seem to be fire extinguishers was done because they wanted a U certificate for the film. They feared that if the Daleks were slaughtering people left, right, and centre with death rays then they might not have the family film they set out to make. Dr Who and the Daleks is a bit too tame for its own good overall. Even in a film aimed at children you have scope to be scarier than Dr Who and the Daleks ever manages to be.

The Daleks are enjoyably colourful though and the inside of the TARDIS is fun and looks like a mad professor's science lab with test tubes and wires everywhere. The scientific goggbleygook dialogue in the script is amusing too. "We've been working on TARDIS for many years. This is the final component. You are privileged, young man, to be the first visitor to our time and space machine. There. I can now set the controls for anywhere in time and space that we wish to go. When I push that lever, this room and everything in it will dissolve into their respective component electrical charges. We're all made of thcm! These charges will then be transferred in time and space and reassembled in their proper order and their proper place."

Roy Castle is the comic relief here as Ian Chesterton. This is probably another reason why Doctor Who die-hards may not warm to this film. Ian was played in the television show by William Russell as a heroic and forthright sort of character. Roy Castle's version of Ian is closer to Frank Spencer or Mr Bean than the Ian of the television show. You may find Roy's clowning a bit wearing by the time this film has ended - Amicus offering a more comedic take on Doctor Who than the William Hartnell led television show. Roberta Tovey is great as the Doctor's smart scientific minded young granddaughter. Apparently the director, in order to speed up the production, offered Tovey a shilling every time she successfully did a take in one go and she became so accomplished at this she ended up costing him a small fortune! Jennie Linden is also well cast as Barbara.

Dr Who and the Daleks is no masterpiece but it's a lively and well made children's film with some amusing moments and fun production design. It's the sort of thing you'd watch half-asleep on a Sunday afternoon and perfectly passable if one's expectations aren't unduly high. One unavoidable problem the film has from a modern perspective is that the Daleks have been done to death in the television show and have lost a lot of their novelty and mystique as a consequence. It was rather like Start Trek - where they wheeled the Borg back out so many times you got bored of them in the end. Still, in 1965 that wasn't the case and children in Britain were more than happy to see the Daleks on the big screen in glorious colour. One might even venture that the Amicus Doctor Who films, while hardly classics, are a trifle underrated. Perhaps if they'd made them canon and Peter Cushing's Doctor was an alien Time Lord they might have a better reputation?

THE SKULL (1965)

The Skull was directed by Freddie Francis and written by Milton Subotsky. It is based on the short story by Robert Bloch - The Skull of the Marquis de Sade. The story was first published in 1945 as part of the anthology Weird Tales. The story explores themes of obsession, the power of influence, and the darkest aspects of human nature. Freddie Francis said that much of Subotsky's original script was not much more than an outline and had to be rewritten (by Francis himself) while they were shooting the film. The Skull is the first non-compendium horror film made by Amicus and feels a lot like a Hammer film at times - which was probably the intention. Amicus making a Hammer style film was a sign of growing confidence and a belief that they could beat that legendary studio at their own game. But was this confidence justified by the actual film? Well, let's find out.

The story in The Skull revolves around an antiques collector named Christopher Maitland (Peter Cushing - by now an Amicus regular) who has a particular interest in rare and unusual objects of the occult. Maitland is offered the chance to possess the skull of the Marquis de Sade by the dodgy dealer Marco (Patrick Wymark). It transpires that the skull was stolen from Maitland's friend Sir Matthew Phillips (Christopher Lee). Phillips was very happy to be rid of it though for this dangerous and devilish skull is cursed and seems to spell madness and doom for anyone who dares to come into contact with it. "All I can say to you is keep away from the skull of the Marquis de Sade!" The unwitting

Maitland is about to find this all out for himself. Never meddle with things you don't understand in horror films. It can only lead to trouble. Will Maitland be able to offer any resistance to the diabolical curse of the skull?

The Skull is an absorbing and wonderfully acted horror film with a terrific cast of actors. Although it is boosted by a strange and atmospheric score by Elisabeth Lutyens, one of the interesting things about the film is the way too that it also isn't afraid of silence. There are long scenes and sequences that play out with just Cushing onscreen alone and they are all very compelling. This is definitely a film you should never casually watch as something on in the background. You have to always pay close attention and watch each and every scene because parts of the story are conveyed in a very visual way with little to no dialogue.

One clever touch in The Skull is the way that the film begins in the 1800s with the grave of the Marquis de Sade plundered and said graverobber then meeting a nasty end for his trouble. We therefore assume this is going to be a period film that mimics Hammer but once this prologue ends we move to the present day with Cushing's antiques collector. It's a nice little way to whip the rug out from under the expectations of the viewer. Amicus show us they are perfectly capable of making a Hammer horror type of film but then quickly move away and give us something slightly different. The 'present day' in the film feels enjoyably anachronistic though, a quality which Amicus and British horror films of this vintage in general often have.

Once in the present day, the focus of the story is Peter Cushing and he's very good in this film as you would expect. It's nice to have an Amicus film where Cushing is the lead in what is a relatively 'straight' role. Maitland isn't an eccentric or a doddery old man. He's quite a thoughtful and intelligent man but fairly normal. Just Cushing sitting alone and quietly musing on this puzzling mystery in his occult antique and book strewn home is great fun. I would love to live in Maitland's house from The Skull. It looks like an ancient but stylish and very cosy Victorian book shop. Cushing always engages our curiosity in the story and is also believably terrified when the skull begins to exert its dark powers. As a character, Maitland (Milton Subotsky was strangely obsessed with the name 'Maitland' wasn't he?) is a good window through which the story is told.

Christopher Lee, in a glorified cameo, only has a few scenes in the film but he makes the most of them and it's always a pleasure to see Cushing and Lee together onscreen. Look out for the scene where they seem to having a frame of snooker (or billiards perhaps). You can tell that Christopher Lee is no Jimmy White. The shot he plays is terrible! There's a fun scene too at the start of The Skull where Lee's character begins making ludicrously over inflated bids at an auction - much to the bafflement of Maitland. You could easily imagine Lee and Cushing swapping roles in The Skull and both being equally effective. It's nice though to have Cushing as the lead here as he often played the supporting role of the friend in many of these types of films.

The highlight of the film comes when the curse of the skull starts to have grave consequences for Cushing and exert a hypnotic trippy effect of bizarre nightmarish imagery. Maitland is arrested (by patently bogus policemen) and put through a surreal Kafkaesque ordeal full of nightmare fuel. It's great stuff. The scene where Cushing is arrested and sits in the back of a car with these sullen heavies who claim to be detectives is very good too. The Skull is quite constrictive and mostly plays out in a few rooms and buildings but it doesn't really matter because the intimate nature of the piece is very compelling. This is one horror film where the budget (and, as we know, Amicus never had a huge amount of money to juggle with when it came to making films) isn't a problem as there are not really any monsters or elaborate set designs and special effects in The Skull.

There are some great little cameos in The Skull that make it even more cultish and enjoyable. Michael Gough appears as an auctioneer at the start and the barking mad Patrick Magee has a small part as a police doctor. Magee only has a few scenes but it's great to see him anyway. Nigel Green (of Zulu fame) also has a few cameo appearances as a stern by the book police inspector investigating the strange events that abound in the wake of the skull. Patrick Wymark is also good as Marco. Wymark was in many great films like Repulsion, Where Eagles Dare, and Witchfinder General. He sadly died in 1970 at the young age of 44.

Look out for Peter Woodthorpe too as Bert Travers. Woodthorpe later played Del Boy's dad Reg Trotter in an episode of Only Fools and Horses. This was the 1983 episode Thicker than Water. Woodthorpe was only nine years older than David Jason too! Trivia you will never need - Peter Woodthorpe was the voice of Pigsy in the dubbed version of the cult Japanese action show Monkey. British kids in the early 1980s used to watch Monkey on Friday teatime.

The last act of The Skull is enjoyably strange and delirious as the frazzled Maitland feels the full brunt of the curse. Those shots of Cushing 'through' the perspective of the skull are a little hokey but great fun. What helps The Skull too is that the film is only 83 minutes long so it never really threatens to outstay its welcome and something that can watched quite easily even if you don't have a lot of spare time. I gather the relative skimpiness of the running time was down to the fact that the script was written on the hoof at the last minute and so not exactly the weightiest of tomes. These teething troubles are not evident in the actual film though. The finished product never betrays the fact that it was a slightly troubled pre-production.

The Skull is a good little horror picture that is a must watch for Cushing fans - and who isn't a fan of Peter Cushing? This was apparently the first film where Cushing and Christopher Lee play friends who have a long history together. As they were friends in real life their onscreen chemistry is as authentic as you would expect. The only possible drawback for some with The Skull might be the slow burn nature of the mystery and the lack of spectacle and blood. Those who do appreciate the slow pacing and use of silence will find much to enjoy though in this film though. The Skull is a very enjoyable little horror mystery and is all the more enjoyable for the leading part it affords the great Peter Cushing.

THE PSYCHOPATH (1966)

The Psychopath was directed by Freddie Francis and written by Robert Bloch. This is sometimes said to be Amicus veering into Italian giallo territory but if anything it is more of a killer doll caper with a slab of Psycho - all with mixed results it has to be said. Robert Bloch didn't like this film very much and complained about the penny pinching of Amicus. To be fair to Amicus it wasn't so much that they were Scrooge but more the fact they didn't have much money to make these films. Milton Subotsky and Max Rosenberg were not Cubby Broccoli and Harry Saltzman making Bond films. They had tight budgets and a bit of penny pinching was unavoidable.

Amicus never made anything else quite like this again but the film was rather popular in Europe and seems to draw fairly decent retrospective reviews whenever it is mentioned these days. The plot of The Psychopath has a series of strange murders abounding. The murders are of men who play in a string quartet together and a creepy toy doll is left at the scene of each death. But what connects these men besides this? Something dark and dodgy in the secret dim and distant past I'll wager. Inspector Holloway (Patrick Wymark) investigates and is soon very curious about a certain Mrs Von Sturm (Margaret Johnston) - an eccentric woman who lives in a strange house full of dolls with her irritable son Mark (John Standing).

The Psychopath is a film with some interesting elements that never completely manages to mesh together in a satisfying way. You might say that The Psychopath is less than the sum of its parts. The basic plot is engaging enough - with the toy dolls adding an enjoyably bizarre note to each of the murders. Red herrings seem to abound too and we suspect two or three people before we settle on the real culprit. One might argue that the film is too obvious though in this regard. It doesn't really surprise us in any way at the end. The film still has a fair way to go by the time we've already worked out who the murderer was. You always feel like this film's third act could have been a lot twistier than it actually turns out to be. The mystery is never really made as opaque as it could have been.

This is a rather cheap and drab looking film at times but maybe that's deliberate and more fitting with this particular genre? It does seem to be aiming for a shadow strewn downbeat look at times. The gothic nature of Mrs Von Sturm's house is quite effective. I like the scene where Inspector Holloway goes to talk to her and can barely make her out amidst all the dolls in her living room. It makes for a great little scene as he peers over the dolls desperately trying to work out where the human voice in this surreal room full of toys is coming from.

There are a few scenes in a junkyard and lots of interiors. You don't get too much in the way of location work in The Psychopath. When one character is murdered it looks as if they quickly shot the scene in the Shepperton car park or something. The characters frequently visit this swanky restaurant too but it's so obviously just a small studio set that they don't even have windows or a kitchen in the restaurant. You never quite get a sense that this film is taking place in something that feels like the real world. It always feels studio bound and slightly fake. One might argue (again) though that this quality is deliberate.

Thankfully, the cast in the film is interesting and - in some cases - rather eccentric. Patrick Wymark is pretty good as the inspector but his performance is very restrained all things considered. He doesn't really let loose or have fun in the way that Alfred Marks did in Scream and Scream Again or Donald Pleasance also did respectively in Death Line, both in similar roles as police inspectors. Marks and Pleasance seemed like they were improvising and having fun but Wymark goes in the opposite direction and underplays the part. I did enjoy the moment though where Wymark abruptly leaves a colleague in the restaurant. "Someone has to settle the bill. It's bound to be outrageous." Wymark is quite a dry, world weary presence in the film and this 'hardboiled' aspect to his character is effective.

Margaret Johnston, by contrast, shows no restraint when it comes to her character. Her performance is gloriously bonkers as the toy doll obsessed Mrs Von Sturm. The scenery chewing of Johnston doesn't harm the film in the slightest. If anything, it gives The Psychopath some hammy fun and energy that it probably needs. John Standing is also quite eccentric as Von Sturm's son. He's sort of set up to be Norman Bates at the start (Inspector Holloway clearly pegs him as the first possible suspect) although his character is an absolute chatterbox compared to Norman Bates. Standing seems to be permanently outraged by everything in the film. If you made him a nice cup of tea he'd probably be theatrically offended that you didn't pick the right biscuits. This gives his performance quite an amusing and entertaining quality. Robert Crewdson also seems to be in an eccentric film of his own as a sculptor. There are some really weird performances in The Psychopath.

The two young leads (though Wymark gets the Lion's share of the screen time) in the film are Judy Huxtable and Don Borisenko. Huxtable (who didn't have a long acting career and is most famous for being the former wife of Peter Cook) and Borisenko (a Canadian actor who worked a lot in Britain around this time but never became very famous - his IMDB credits end in 1973) are both dull and given precious little to do. The film grinds to a halt whenever these two are onscreen and has you pining for the bonkers Margaret Johnston or her strange and highly irritable son to come back again. You half suspect they only cast Judy Huxtable so they could put her on the poster. I'd argue that in terms of the cast, Harold Lang actually steals the show from everyone in a brief appearance as a (obviously gay) toy shop owner who with a nice turn of phrase and an encyclopedic knowledge of dolls. It's a shame that Lang doesn't feature more in the film as he's great.

The score by Elisabeth Lutyens makes a good eerie backdrop to the intrigue onscreen and though parts of The Psychopath work very well it's also messy in other places and never really makes a coherent or completely satisfying thriller. It's a brave attempt though to make something a little bit different and fans of outrageously over the top horror acting should have some fun at least. The Psychopath is not as satisfying as it could have been but this eccentric thriller is an interesting change of pace for Amicus. If you have a weakness for killer doll antics (and who doesn't?) then you should manage to get some enjoyment out of this film even if it never really threatens to become one of the more memorable films that Amicus made.

DALEKS' INVASION EARTH 2150 A.D (1966)

Daleks' Invasion Earth 2150 A.D. is the second and last of the Amicus Doctor Who films and was again directed by Gordon Flemyng and written by Milton Subotsky (though it seems that David Whitaker once again worked on the screenplay and was likely the real author). The story in Daleks' Invasion Earth 2150 A.D. is based on the Doctor Who television serial The Dalek Invasion of Earth. Peter Cushing and Roberta Tovey reprise their roles as the Doctor and his grandaughter Susan respectively. Cushing apparently said he would only do this film is they asked Roberta Tovey to come back too - which was a very sweet gesture on his part. Jennie Linden and Roy Castle are not in this sequel though because they were unavailable this time around.

They planned to make a trilogy of these Amicus Doctor Who films but Daleks' Invasion Earth 2150 A.D. turned out to be the last outing for Peter Cushing's Doctor. The box-office returns of Daleks' Invasion Earth 2150 A.D. (which had a bigger budget than the first film) were not deemed sufficient to do another one. It appears that the public demand for more big screen Dalek capers was already waning and so Amicus decided to get out of the Doctor Who racket. The general perception is that this film is a definite improvement on Dr Who and the Daleks. Daleks' Invasion Earth 2150 A.D. is less constrictive than the first film with a bigger scope and more outdoor locations. It also more atmospheric than the first film and generally more entertaining. Daleks' Invasion Earth 2150 A.D. isn't entirely bereft though of the some of the shortcomings the first film had.

Peter Cushing seemed to like these two films and had some warm reflections on his time as the Doctor in a 1990s interview. "I had played Winston Smith in 1984 on television, and the next thing I played Doctor Who. I was doing it in the cinema while Bill Hartnell was doing it on TV! That's the way it goes. It was no surprise to me to learn that the first Doctor Who film was in the top twenty box office hits of 1965, despite the panning the critics gave us. That's why they made the sequel and why they spent twice as much money on it. Those films are among my favourites because they brought me popularity with younger children. They'd say their parents didn't want to meet me in a dark alley but Doctor Who changed that. After all, he is one of the most heroic and successful parts an actor can play. That's one of the main reasons the series had such a long run on TV. I am very grateful for having been part of such a success story."

Daleks' Invasion Earth 2150 A.D. has a new comic relief companion as Roy Castle is replaced by Bernard Cribbins as a policeman named Tom Campbell. Tom ends up in the TARDIS when he mistakes it for a real police box. An easy mistake to make from the outside I'd imagine! Jill Curzon also joins the cast as the Doctor's niece Louise. The premise of the film has the TARDIS shuttling through time and space again and ending up in the year 2150 where it transpires that the Daleks have invaded Earth. Watford is now overrun by Daleks. I love the idea that the Daleks have invaded Earth and their main focus and primary objective was Watford! Anyway, the Daleks have started turning humans into brainwashed 'Robomen' and England seems to be a pile of rubble ruled over by its deadly new pepperpot masters. The Daleks are intent on using the Earth's core to create a giant spaceship and - as ever - it will be to the Doctor and his plucky companions to put a stop to their nefarious plans.

Daleks' Invasion Earth 2150 A.D. is largely more of the same that you got with Dr Who and the Daleks. If you didn't like the first one then this second slice of Amicus Dr Who probably won't convert you but if you did enjoy the original you might actually like this sequel more. This film is more eventful and action packed and the plot is more fun. It's just as colourful as the first film and the special effects are better too. The flying saucer in the film especially is really good and quite eerie too. If you love old school special effects with models and miniatures you'll have a lot of fun with Daleks' Invasion Earth 2150 A.D. If you ask me the old school special effects in Daleks' Invasion Earth 2150 A.D. are much more realistic and scary than some of the stuff you get in these headache inducing modern CG films.

There's a lot of humour in the film (something the television show wasn't really known for at the time but would adopt more of in later decades) and Bernard Cribbins is given numerous slapstick sequences in the film. Cribbins is fun though and his antics stave off any potential lulls (even if they do occasionally threaten to overstay their welcome). Bernard Cribbins would of course memorably join the cast of the televison series (in the David Tennant era) as 'Wilf' decades later. Look out for Ray Brooks in this film too as a resistance leader. Brooks was coming off the success of The Knack ...and How to Get It - which was directed by Richard Lester. Andrew Keir, who would play Professor Bernard Quatermass in Hammer's classic 1967 film Quatermass and the Pit, is also in the cast of Daleks' Invasion Earth 2150 A.D. as Wyler. You may recognise Philip Madoc, who plays Brockley in Daleks' Invasion Earth 2150 A.D. Madoc played the German U-boat captain in the "Don't tell him Pike!" episode of Dad's Army.

While these Amicus Doctor Who films are never the most serious of endeavours, the frantic pace and enthusiastic performances of the cast help to carry it all along. Happily, you always get the impression that everyone is doing their best to give you a good time. You certainly couldn't accuse Bernard Cribbins of phoning in his performance. Peter Cushing was apparently not in the best of health when this film was made and was absent for early shooting so the supporting characters get more screen time here than they might have done otherwise. I suspect we got a lot more of the slapstick antics of Bernard Cribbins than was originally planned as a consequence.

Peter Cushing is slightly less of the 'doddery old man' than he was in the first one but his Doctor is still not the most serious interpretation you've even seen of this legendary part. He's fun though. He's not playing the 'lonely god' angsty Doctor that we later got in the television series (nor indeed is he playing the grumpy Bill Hartnell Doctor) so if you just accept that Cushing is playing a different sort of character, a grandfather inventor, then his performance is fine.

The science in Daleks' Invasion Earth 2150 A.D. is somewhat dodgy to say the least but then these films are supposed to be for children. You'll notice, by the way, that despite being set in the year 2150, the buildings and vehicles in the film all look very 1950s and 1960s! I suppose futuristic cars and buildings would have been too time consuming and costly to fully convey. Nitpicks aside, this film is good undemanding Saturday morning fun for younger viewers with plenty of explosions, humour, outdoor location work, special effects, and intrigue. I would say this is a marked improvement over the first film with its bigger budget and less constrictive aura.

As we have mentioned, Milton Subotsky planned to make a third Amicus Doctor Who film but ultimately this never transpired in the end. The two Doctor Who films he did make are not everyone's cup of tea and don't have much in common with the television show but as relics of the Swinging Sixties and artefacts of British sci-fi cinema and family entertainment they are agreeable enough diversions and, despite their flaws, have a lot more charm than most modern films of this ilk.

Speaking personally, I would much rather watch Dr Who and the Daleks and Daleks' Invasion Earth 2150 A.D. than, say, the Star Wars prequels or CG blockbuster rubbish like the Transformers franchise, Independence Day: Resurgence, and the new Jurassic Park films. You could plausibly say there was a missed opportunity by Amicus because the legacy of these Doctor Who films would be greater and more enduring if they'd been extensions of the television show with William Hartnell as the lead, but, taken for purely on their own terms, Dr Who and the Daleks and Daleks' Invasion Earth 2150 A.D. are decent fun and could have been a lot worse.

THE DEADLY BEES (1966)

The Deadly Bees was directed by Freddie Francis and written by Robert Bloch and Anthony Marriott. Francis later said that hiring Marriott to rewrite Bloch's script was a mistake. The film is based on HF Heard's 1941 novel A Taste for Honey. The novel is about a lunatic who, as you do, trains an army of intelligent killer bees. This film was actually written for Christopher Lee and Boris Karloff but - sadly - neither were apparently affordable in the end. "I had another title and another concept," said Bloch. "I wanted to stick more closely to the plot of the classic book itself, and wrote the leads for two friends of mine who greatly enjoyed working with one another -- Boris Karloff and Christopher Lee. But again, the budget interfered; there was no money for two stars of such magnitude. And the director brought in another writer to "modernize" the story -- while Milton and Max were away in Europe. The result certainly disappointed me, and I'm told it disappointed Milton and Max, too, but when they returned the production was ready to roll and it was too late to return to the original screenplay."

The Deadly Bees seems very inspired by Alfred Hitchcock's The Birds. Swap killer bees for killer birds and the two films are quite similar. Well, at the very least, you could say they aren't a million miles apart. The plot of The Deadly Bees revolves around a pop singer named Vicki Robbins (Suzanna Leigh). Vicki is suffering from exhaustion and collapses while performing a song on television. Rest and recuperation is the cure. She is packed off to a cottage on Seagull Island to take it easy. At the cottage, she stays with a rather grumpy couple named Ralph and Mary Hargrove (Guy Doleman and Catherine Finn). Ralph is a beekeeper - as is the nearest neighbour Manfred (Frank Finlay). When a spate of killer bee attacks start occurring in the area, Vicki turns sleuth to discover who is responsible. Let the bee mayhem commence!

Killer bee capers. Television films in the seventies were obsessed with killer bees. You had The Savage Bees and Terror Out of the Sky * - not to mention Michael Caine's famously terrible big screen outing The Swarm. You might argue then that The Deadly Bees is - of sorts - the grandfather of this horror subgenre. Sadly, there is one thing that all killer bee movies seem to have in common. None of them are very good. Maybe it's something to do with the fact that bees make terrible villains. Who really has anything against the humble bumble bee? The worst sin of The Deadly Bees is that this is a strangely dull film for most of its running time. It's not the most gripping of horror films. Seagull Island is depicted by a few constrictive farmhouse sets and a couple of outdoor shots where the characters look as if they are on a small farm. This all makes it feel like a rather cramped and visually uninteresting film to look at. The Deadly Bees is one of the cheapest looking of the Amicus horror films.

The story in The Deadly Bees takes far too long to go anywhere (though to be fair to the film it is clearly trying to be a mystery as much as it is a killer bee caper) and the bee attacks are few and far between. They are passable enough when they arrive though. You get close ups of real bees and superimposed footage of swarms placed over the actors. Bits of what look like fluff (I gather they used coffee granules amongst other things to suggest a swarm of bees!) fill up the screen to convey the bee carnage. The special effects are a bit scrappy from a modern perspective but they are likeable and enjoyable because you can appreciate the effort that went into them. When you consider that the people making The Deadly Bees didn't have computers and didn't have much money you'd have to say that they did a decent enough job with the bee shenanigans.

Despite this, you wouldn't say that The Deadly Bees was ever that scary or gripping. One of the problems with these nature run wild sort of horror films is that you become impatient sometimes waiting for the bee (or whatever insect or animal is attacking people) attacks to occur and The Deadly Bees rations them to a frustrating degree.

Much of the film revolves around the sleuthing of Vicki as she befriends Manfred and tries to learn more about Ralph. You don't need to be Lieutenant Columbo though to deduce which of the beekeepers is the real villain. There isn't much of a mystery for the viewer to grapple with. You can't help but wondering too why Vicki doesn't just go home! If I was staying on an island in a farmhouse and killer bees were on the loose I'd be on the first boat out of that place as fast as I could. Vicki often seems remarkably blase in the midst of this pesky bee palava.

What does help The Deadly Bees a lot though is the presence of Suzanna Leigh as the lead. Leigh came into this film straight after starring in Paradise, Hawaiian Style with Elvis. She would go onto to appear in a number of horror films - Lust for a Vampire, The Fiend, Son of Dracula. She was also in the Hammer film The Lost Continent and the Hammer anthology television show Journey into the Unknown. Suzanna Leigh is one of those actors who you feel could have been quite a big star with a bit more luck. She has a likeable relaxed screen presence and was attractive but not in an obvious blonde bimbo sort of way. Suzanna Leigh was only about 20 when she made The Killer Bees but she seems older than that. She just had a certain look and stature that set her apart from other young horror starlets of this era. By the way, I was interested to see that Vicki has an electric toothbrush in the film. I honestly didn't know people used electric toothbrushes in 1966. You learn something new every day!

Guy Doleman (famous for his part in the Harry Palmer films) was a very crisp and polished actor and brings some gravitas to what is a fairly thankless part as Ralph. "It's dangerous to involve yourself in matters you don't understand!" he snaps at one point, as if a mild curiosity about bees is like trying to defuse a nuclear bomb in your shed. One can't help wondering if the grumpiness of Ralph is Doleman's way of cursing his agent for landing him in this film. Frank Finlay is aged up to play Manfred and seems to be quite enjoying himself. There's a playfulness to Finlay in this film absent in the other actors. He knows The Deadly Bees is not going to trouble the Oscar nominations so he's determined to at least have some fun. Hammer stalwart Michael Ripper also pops up as (yes, you guessed it) the landlord of the pub (who, oddly, also seems to be a police officer). When it comes to old horror films, Michael clearly had something of a lock on the pub landlord/tavern keeper parts.

The Deadly Bees, in terms of atmosphere and its anachronistic interiors, often seems to be mimicking Hammer but there are some 'youth culture' trappings at the start. We see a pop group called The Birds with a young Ronnie Wood on guitar. The start of the film in the television studio is a reminder that Amicus were never afraid to be contemporary in their horror films. Hammer, by contrast, were more reticent in this regard. Occasionally, The Deadly Bees takes us away from Seagull Island to some sort of government ministry office where two men discuss letters they've had from a nutty beekeeper who claims to have developed a strain of killer bees. You probably could have lost these scenes without making much difference to the film. They don't feel completely necessary and also have the unfortunate effect of coming across as exposition - as if the audience needs the plot and villain scheme spoon fed to them.

The Deadly Bees has a pretty good cast and is relatively competent but - ultimately - it's never really that interesting or especially scary. You would probably expect an Amicus film about killer bees to be a lot more entertaining and cultish than The Deadly Bees ever manages to be. This one falls a long way short of the Amicus top table and is fairly forgettable - even by the rather low standards of the dreaded killer bee subgenre of horror. The Deadly Bees was the subject of a 1998 episode of Mystery Science Theater 3000, thus perhaps enshrining its reputation as a bad film - or a comical one at least.

I haven't seen that Mystery Science Theater 3000 episode but given that The Deadly Bees is not outrageously terrible (I've seen millions of horror films worse than this) nor especially funny (as in so bad its funny - even the pop band playing at the start are actually quite good!) nor awash with terrible acting (look at that cast!) I'm not exactly sure what they would have found to 'riff' on for 83 minutes. There are only so many bee themed jokes to go around and comic mimicry of the posh English accents would get old pretty fast if you ask me.

I think the main problem with The Deadly Bees isn't that it is an incompetent or laughable film, because it isn't, but more the fact that it is never as much fun as you want it to be. Maybe they should have embraced the daftness much more and really gone for it. That would definitely have given Mystery Science Theater 3000 an easier time. Robert Bloch commented that The Deadly Bees "soon buzzed off into critical oblivion, unwept, unhonoured and unstung" - which is fair enough I suppose. We can only wonder how much better the more serious and faithful film of this story Bloch had intended would have turned out.

* The Savage Bees is a 1976 made for television film directed by Bruce Geller. This is another of the nature run wild thrillers that seemed in vogue in the seventics and as far as the killer bee subgenre goes one of the better examples (although to be honest that isn't saying an awful lot when one considers the competition). The premise has a swarm of African killer bees descending on New Orleans during Mardi Gras. These pesky bees have rampaged through South America and now, thanks to a freighter collision (or something), have their sights set on the United States.

The Savage Bees is surprisingly straight laced for a film about killer bees and bee antics are mostly absent for much of the running time save for the end when we finally get to see a swarm. You've probably seen bigger swarms in your back garden than you see in The Savage Bees. There seems to have been a conspicuous effort here not to make the film too goofy or silly, which is fair enough I suppose, and this is perfectly illustrated by the fact that Michael Parks as a doctor gives a completely restrained and 'normal' performance. Ben Johnson is the Sheriff while Horst Buchholz is the only cast member who threatens to ham it up as a scientist bee expert.

The script includes a decent amount of arcane knowledge about the habits of bees and one senses that they've tried to be accurate as they can in a film of this type as far as the science goes. While this is all quite commendable it does make the film seem a little dry at times and lacking sufficient B-movie action. The location work is very good but the film does have a rather drab and washed out look. The modest budget is illustrated by the freighter collision at the start. They don't have a special effects budget capable of depicting this so they have to imply it more than anything. The lack of bees is apparent but when they do show a swarm gathered around a character's car near the end it's quite effective and tense. The Savage Bees is quite competent with a fairly decent cast but it isn't the most exciting or inventive of the many TV thrillers of this decade and ultimately all plays out in far less entertaining a fashion than one hopes and expects.

Terror Out of the Sky was directed by Lee H Katzin and is a sequel to The Savage Bees. What is it with the seventies and killer bee films? The premise has entomologist Jeannie Devereux (now played by Tovah Feldshuh) having to stop another swarm of African killer bees in California with the help of Doctor David Martin (Efrem Zimbalist Jr). The world probably didn't need a sequel to The Savage Bees but Terror Out of the Sky is not as bad as you might fear. One thing I did like about the film is that it seems to have more bees than the last one - always a bonus in a killer bee film!

One early death with a scientist getting attacked by bees has literally thousands of the rascals on his hazmat suit. I should point out though that I always struggle slightly with the killer bee genre. Bees are always a comforting pleasant presence to me in the summer and I sort of hate to see them as villains. Wasps on the other hand. You could maybe accept them as the baddies more readily. The big setpiece here involves a bus full of children coming under peril and then - later - a heroic act by one of the scientists. These scenes have a lot of bees so you get value for money although they do stretch the bee antics out somewhat. Some stretches of the film are a little on the dull side but the outdoor location work is pleasant enough. It was a shrewd move to make the lead character come from the original film. This means they can craftily insert footage from The Savage Bees as flashback/nightmare sequences.

The cast are serviceable enough but never too much more than that. It's interesting and enjoyable I think to see Efrem Zimbalist Jr, looking like he could be Tovah Feldshuh's grandfather, as the male lead. If they made this film today, Zimbalist's character would be played by some twenty-six year old steroid enhanced catalogue model. Dan Haggerty also has a prominent part as Jeannie's boyfriend and his beard is certainly on fine form. It's hard to tell if Haggerty is bored by the film or simply laid back. Maybe it was a combination of the two. Terror Out of the Sky is generally frowned upon as the terrible sequel to The Savage Bees but I personally didn't notice a huge gulf between the two films. The original is not exactly The Seventh Seal. While this sequel is a little more cornball and formula bound than the first, it has a likeable enough cast and gives you more bee swarm shenanigans (if that's your thing) than its predecessor. It's no classic but not as bad as legend would have it.

THE TERRORNAUTS (1967)

The Terrornauts was directed by Montgomery Tully. Tully was an Irish director who worked on gazillions of low-budget British films. The Terrornauts was written by John Brunner and based on The Wailing Asteroid by Murray Leinster. Milton Subotsky's wife Fiona said she helped get the script treatment for the film finished because everyone at Amicus was a bit overloaded at the time. The plot of the film has Dr Joe Burke (Simon Oates) in charge of a scientific project in England that listens out for alien signals and signs of extraterrestrial life in the great void of space. His team consists of electronics expert Ben Keller (Stanley Meadows) and office manager Sandy Lund (Zena Marshall). They haven't had much luck though in their search for alien signals and are frequently annoyed too by their penny pinching manager Henry Shore (Max Adrian) sticking his beak into their affairs.

Shore wants to shut the operation down if they don't get any quick results (which seems a bit harsh as they are trying to find evidence of alien life - not exactly the easiest of tasks!) and he's even brought in a fussy accountant named Mr Yellowlees (Charles Hawtrey) to look over the books and make sure they aren't wasting any money. Well, to cut a long story short, Dr Burke's team receive an unexpected signal from an asteroid and are beamed up to a spacecraft in their transmitter shed. Joining them for this unexpected ride in outer space are Mr Yellowlees and the tea lady Mrs Jones (Patricia Hayes). What in the name of Gerry Anderson will happen to our plucky band of scientists?

The Terrornauts has a reputation as a famously bad Amicus film. It is often compared to the films of Ed Wood and one can see how this film has ended up as a frequent suggestion for Mystery Science Theater 3000 to 'riff' upon. The film it seems slightly reminiscent of is This Island Earth *, which DID end up on Mystery Science Theater 3000 - despite being a good film! However, This Island Earth, while silly, did have beautiful production design and impressive special effects for its era. The Terrornauts quite patently does not have any money at all at its disposal. Daleks' Invasion Earth 2150 A.D. had three or times the budget of The Terrornauts and you can see the difference. Most of The Terrornauts takes place in the transmitter room (which looks like something left over from the Dr Who films). There are so few locations you could probably have done this film as a stage play!

The Terrornauts seems quite obviously designed at times to be a comic sci-fi film. In fact, I think people sometimes miss the point of this film when they talk about how bad it is. The Terrornauts was made primarily for children. Despite the lurid poster art this film is - spiritually - closer to Button Moon than Alien! Button Moon was a British children's television programme that aired from 1980 to 1988. The show was created by Ian Allen and narrated by Robin Parkinson. Button Moon followed the adventures of Mr Spoon, his wife Mrs Spoon, and their daughter Tina Teaspoon. Each episode featured the family travelling to Button Moon in their homemade rocket ship. Once on Button Moon, they would explore the various objects and characters they encountered. The show was unique in its use of everyday household items as characters and props. The show's set was also made entirely of cardboard, giving it a distinct visual style. That is basically how I would describe The Terrornauts. A whimsical piece of fluff held together by teapots and cardboard!

This is assuredly not a horror sci-fi and the addition of Charles Hawtrey to the cast indicates this was a vague attempt to go back to the family friendly formula of the Doctor Who films. One thing that does help The Terrornauts somewhat though is the cast. Simon Oates, a tall and urbane actor who nearly played James Bond in the early seventies (Oates once said that he was supposed to play 007 in Diamonds Are Forever but this was scuppered when United Artists persuaded Sean Connery to come back at the last minute), is far too good for this nonsense but to his credit he never really sends up the part or looks too bored. He's actually quite good in the film and has a likeable screen presence that makes you wish he'd been in a few more films (Oates was probably best known for his role in the ecological sci-fi television series Doomwatch).

Zena Marshall, the improbably glamorous office manager in The Terrornauts, played Miss Taro in the first Bond film Dr No. The Terronauts was actually the last screen credit for Marshall as she retired from acting after this. I do hope The Terronauts wasn't to blame for her decision! Charles Hawtrey - on loan it seems from the Carry On series - also turns up as the comic relief. Hawtrey plays a similar (if less outrageous) sort of character in The Terrornauts to his Carry On roles and is an enjoyable enough presence, steering the film through a few lulls with his comic reactions. Patricia Hayes is fun too as the tea lady caught up in the mayhem and Max Adrian from Dr Terror's House of Horrors seems to enjoying himself as the bad tempered boss of the scientists.

The Terrornauts does struggle with its modest budget, especially when they encounter the aliens. The characters are mostly confined to a metallic room once they've been beamed up and meet a robot that looks like it was made from television aerials and saucepans. There is also an alien creature wearing the most unconvincing rubber monster suit you'll ever see. The last third of The Terrornauts is rather hokey at the best of times. When we get an outdoor alien world it is depicted by a quarry with a couple of fake looking planets and suns stuck in the sky. They look like they've been stuck on the frame with blue tac.

This is clearly not a very good film but, strangely, it is quite likeable all the same. You have that enjoyable cast and (in the first half of the film anyway) an earnestness that is charming in its own way. This is a film that sometimes can't decide if it is silly or trying to be a 'straight' sci-fi adventure. It does neither very well but the unwitting middle ground it occasionally treads is watchable enough. When it does spill over into pure nonsense (with the less than convincing special effects) The Terrornauts actually becomes rather entertaining. It's good for a laugh and, at the very least, not many films can claim to have Miss Taro and Charles Hawtrey in the cast together.

If you had to describe The Terrornauts to someone who had never seen it before, you might venture that this is somewhat like watching a British version of that old television show Lost in Space with the special effects budget of Button Moon. Lost in Space was more fun than The Terrornauts ever manages to be but that's as good a description as any for this strange and very forgotten Amicus sci-fi oddity. It might be a silly film but personally I'd rather watch The Terronauts than They Came from Beyond Space (which we'll review next) if given a choice. The Terrornauts is modest fun in a daft sort of way and it is this quality which gives it some charm despite the very evident flaws.

* This Island Earth was directed by Joseph Newman and based on the novel by Raymond F Jones. This is a classic example of a superb bad film. The science is all over the place, the characters and performances are sometimes unintentionally comical, but it looks amazing, a Technicolour Space Opera epic that captures the flamboyance of pulp science fiction stories perhaps more than any other film from this era with the exception of Forbidden Planet. This Island Earth was so expensive to produce that films like this at the time were a rarity and understandably far more troublesome and costly to make than the (soon to be familiar) black and white monster in lonely desert approach to fifties science fiction.

The absurd grandeur and imagination on show makes one forget the shortcomings of This Island Earth (which are sort of charming anyway) and while this is clearly nowhere near as a great a film as the following year's other fifties Technicolour space opera epic Forbidden Planet, the ambition displayed in the Metaluna scenes always makes it very likeable and entertaining. You get psychedelic flying saucers and a pretty good "man in a monster suit" alien mutant with an insect like appearance and a giant brain. A bonkers spectacle of colour and nonsense dazzles the screen. This Island Earth is perhaps a little underrated in the pantheon of vintage science fiction films and despite the ample scope for ridicule it deserves much more than being mere fodder for Mystery Science Theater 3000. The tepid romantic scenes between Reason and Faith Domergue are dull and it takes a while to get going but this film remains visually stunning and a lot of fun in the end.

THEY CAME FROM BEYOND SPACE (1967)

They Came from Beyond Space was directed by Freddie Francis and written by Milton Subotsky (based on the book The Gods Hate Kansas by Joseph Millard). They Came from Beyond Space was shown on a double-bill with The Terrornauts. The Terrornauts was only 75 minutes long and They Came from Beyond Space is not exactly Lord of the Rings either at a concise 85 minutes. What is the plot of They Came from Beyond Space? Strange glowing meteorites land in a field in Cornwall and anyone who comes close to them is taken over by some sort of alien mind control force. The authorities are soon investigating in this most puzzling mystery and hopes will come to rest on American scientist Dr Curtis Temple (Robert Hutton). Temple has a metal plate in his head as a result of a car accident and is therefore immune to the alien mind control. But what do these pesky alien visitors really want?

You might feel a pang of deja vu watching They Came from Beyond Space, given its similarities to many other sci-fi horror films and television shows - although the story on which this film is based came out in 1941 and therefore predates them. That said, it's obvious that They Came from Beyond Space owes something to 1953's It Came From Outer Space and the original classic Invasion of the Body Snatchers. What it owes even more to is the Quatermass series - specifically Quatermass II *. The plots are almost identical. In both They Came from Beyond Space and Quatermass II, meteorites fall in rural England, affect the local population, and secrecy and intrigue becomes rife with the locals acting strangely and some sort of clandestine project in the countryside abounding. One might argue too that They Came from Beyond Space also owes something to an Outer Limits episode called Corpus Earthling **.

They Came from Beyond Space definitely feels like Freddie Francis marking time and paying a few bills. The director never feels that engaged by his task here. He keeps the film moving at a decent pace but there are few memorable images and scenes that lodge in the memory. Francis apparently complained about the non existent budget of They Came from Beyond Space and said that Amicus had no money for this film because they spent it all making The Terrornauts around the same time. Well, I have seen The Terrornauts and there is precious little evidence of a budget in that film either! I think they made BOTH of these films with a non-existent budget. One might argue that Amicus bit off more than they could chew by making a couple of sci-fi films at this juncture considering that they clearly had very modest finances available to make them.

There is no getting away from the fact that They Came from Beyond Space looks quite cheap at times for a sci-fi film. They deploy that old trick beloved of British films and TV shows of yesteryear of shooting scenes in what looks like an abandoned airfield to keep the costs down while still suggesting some sort of military/scientific base. The special effects and props are rather hokey (and recycled from the Doctor Who film) and there are lots of scenes in the countryside and little villages rather than sets and sci-fi trappings to also keep the costs down. Still, the outdoor location work and old cars lends the film a certain charm to modern eyes. At least they actually did a lot of location stuff. A problem with The Deadly Bees is that even when the actors were supposed to be outside they were clearly in a studio but that isn't the case so much here.

They Came from Beyond Space is sort of like watching an episode of The Avengers at times with the countryside scenes and infiltration of the secret base. The only difference being that The Avengers was fun and tongue-in-cheek with witty dialogue. You get none of that irreverence in They Came from Beyond Space and the performances are rather stilted and wooden. Robert Hutton is a very dull leading man and Jennifer Jayne (from the Donald Sutherland segment of Dr Terror's House of Horrors) is sadly turned into a mind controlled alien slave far too soon. It would have been more fun to have her as the female lead investigating the mystery with Hutton.

The unintentional laughs come from Hutton making a special device to block the alien mind control. So you have characters wearing what looks like a colander on their head. Not only can they now thwart alien mind control they can also handily drain pasta and vegetables when it's time for dinner. Joking aside, you have to give the film credit for at least trying to prevent the viewer from becoming bored. There's a car chase (with terrible back projection of the era), fist fights, some charming old school special effects rockets. I like too the fog bound scenes at night when Hutton investigates the countryside. Freddie Francis, despite a production budget that would struggle to pay for a packet of Wotsits and a can of Tizer, at least tried to keep the film moving along at a fair clip.

Things perk up somewhat at the end when Michael Gough appears and plays one of the alien leaders. Gough wears a fluorescent cape and reads his lines as if he's in Hamlet. It's great fun to see Gough hammily thesping up this ridiculous part his agent has landed him. Maybe this film would be more cultish if it had embraced this sort of camp much earlier in the running time. It feels like a slog at times to get through They Came from Beyond Space despite all of the intrigue and incident that the story throws our way. For some reason, this film never really grabs hold of you.

This last part of the film is most obvious in the way that it recycles some sets from the Amicus Doctor Who films. It's also virtually the only part of the part that feels like science fiction (as silly as the science fiction might be here). The scenes at the start - which you might also argue are more traditionally sci-fi - where characters are brainwashed by the glowing meteorites are unavoidably silly. Freddie Francis just can't make these scenes work at all. We've seen this sort of doppelgänger sci-fi thriller about loss of identity done better too many times in other films and even television shows.

They Came from Beyond Space is not a very good film and fairly cheapjack and forgettable as far as these types of old sci-fi films go but it has just enough to make it worth watching at least once (and in recent years at least a much better print has been issued - cleaning up the film considerably and making the dark gloomier scenes with grainy edges much more vibrant and colourful). I doubt this is a film you'd feel like returning to very much though and it always feel somewhat like a diluted Quatermass with no Nigel Kneale. All in all, They Came from Beyond Space is probably one for the Amicus completist more than anything. It's watchable but don't expect Invasion of the Body Snatchers.

The Terrornauts was sort of charming and good for a few laughs but They Came from Beyond Space, sadly, too often feels like a chore rather than a fun experience.

* 1965's Quatermass II is a six-part television series by Nigel Kneale. This was the second Quatermass TV venture and happily - unlike the first - all the episodes remain in existence today for us to watch. The story has Professor Bernard Quatermass (John Robinson) of the British Experimental Rocket Group investigating strange meteorite fragments that keep falling in a rural area of England. Quatermass discovers that a nearby village has been destroyed and a huge industrial plant has been built on the site. The plant is heavily guarded by men in sinister black military uniforms and secrecy abounds. Not only that but the locals and those in positions of power are beginning to act strangely and show signs of a distinctive mark on their face. What can it all mean?

This seems very much like a British version of Invasion of the Body Snatchers (and similar alien invasion paranoia films) and although technically quite primitive today, Quatermass II is very absorbing and draws you into the mystery that slowly unfolds. Nigel Kneale taps into real world fears of the era like the Cold War, bureaucracy, new technology, atomic weapons, and suspicion of outsiders (one would presume that with Britain absorbing large numbers of immigrants from the Commonwealth to plug the post-war shortage of workers this was a very topical theme). "It was 1955, an uncomfortable time," said Kneale. "There was much public concern about a new brand of bureaucracy, which manifested itself in the form of secret establishments: giant radars reputed to endanger human life and concealed huge plastic pods; germ warfare establishments behind barbed wire; atom-proof shelters for chosen administrators."

This series is unavoidably dated in terms of the production (do not not expect Star Wars when the action moves to space in the last episode) with the acting very theatrical indeed and a few flubbed lines here and there but the strength of the story mitigates the rough around the edges elements - especially the early scenes in the countryside. If you watch a lot of British horror and science fiction you quickly realise that the English countryside is never a place to be trusted. Perhaps a lot of the horror and sci-fi writers bought remote cottages and used ancient myths and local legends to stir their imaginations!

The lead role is played by an actor named John Robinson and he's decent enough if probably not the greatest of the Quatermass thespians. Robinson is rather stagey - like most of the cast as a whole. Television was a new medium for actors at the time and it seems like the cast here are not quite in tune with the camera setup and precise cues required. No one is distractingly awful though and it's impressive the way they juggle such a large cast and ambitious story on what must have been a very modest budget. The story has some chilling moments as the veil is slowly pulled back on the grand masterplan and - as ever with vintage television - the black and white seems to add a certain eerie ambiance. With each episode clocking in at under half an hour it will not take too long to rattle through through these and they remain very enjoyable.

** Corpus Earthling is an old black and white episode of The Outer Limits. In the story, scientist Dr Paul Cameron (Robert Culp) suffers a head injury and has a steel plate inserted as a consequence. When he returns back to work he hears what seems to be two rock specimens in his lab talking to each other and revealing they are aliens in rock form planning to take over the world. Only Cameron can hear the voices though. No one else can. Has he gone insane or are the rocks really talking to each other and sentient?

Corpus Earthling is one of the most fondly remembered Outer Limits episodes and a lot of fun once it gets going. The early premise alone is enough to keep us watching. Talking rocks that seem to be aliens! This episode riffs on The Invasion of the Body Snatchers - with the rocks apparently able to manipulate and control other people, leading Cameron to have to work out who is (or isn't) themselves anymore. Cameron decides to have a holiday in Mexico to see if this helps his rather frazzled state of mind. However, this vacation only serves to confirm his fears. The alien rocks have taken over scientist Dr Temple and he is soon in hot pursuit.

What's great about this episode is the way that it starts with constrictive lab locations and then almost becomes a road movie of sorts with the desert locations as the action to moves to Mexico. It makes the episode feel quite expansive and by presenting us with fresh backdrops makes the story more interesting in a visual sense. There is a lot of scope to the story in the way that it opens out and moves beyond the laboratory interiors. Many episodes of The Outer Limits feel like B-horror movies. Obviously, this can be both a blessing and a curse. B-movies can be wonderful but they can also be deadly dull. Corpus Earthling is definitely in the former camp. Happily, this is a great example of The Outer Limits as a fun B-horror movie experience. What could be more B-movie than malevolent rocks? One might add too that there is nothing B-movie about the acting, music, and cinematography of Corpus Earthling. In all of these fields this episode - and The Outer Limits generally - is terrific. One could argue that Corpus Earthling is the scariest of all Outer Limits episodes and it contains some very dark imagery. Barry Atwater is absolutely terrifying when he's taken over, transformed into a relentless zombie. That's another great thing about Corpus Earthling. The way it turns into a zombie yarn - and this years (and even decades) before zombies became so familiar to us in film and television.

TORTURE GARDEN (1967)

It is high time we had some more Amicus horror anthology capers isn't it? After sitting through They Came from Beyond Space it's the least we deserve. Amicus returned to the horror portmanteau with 1967's Torture Garden. The second Amicus anthology film drew on stories by Psycho author Robert Bloch. The finance for the film was supplied by Columbia (who stumped up half a million quid - which was big money for Amicus) and at their request Jack Palance and Burgess Meredith were signed to give the film more appeal in North America. The Emmy award winning and Oscar nominated Palance and the popular Meredith, who was well known to American audiences through his appearances in Rod Serling's The Twilight Zone *, were shrewd additions to the cast when it came to marketing this film in the United States.

Christopher Lee was absent as the part he was earmarked for was taken by Jack Palance but Peter Cushing does return. Don Banks and James Bernard supply the score and Freddie Francis returned to direct again. The film was a financial success and confirmation that the decision by Amicus to return to compendium horror was the correct one. Torture Garden was only the second of the Amicus compendiums but it always feels slightly like the lost forgotten one to me. The other Amicus portmanteau films seem to be more fondly remembered. It might have something to do with Torture Garden feeling slightly less British and more generic at times than its Amicus stablemates. It isn't quite as much fun as the other films for some reason.

The wraparound framing device features a strange circus sideshow run by a showman named Dr Diabolo (Burgess

Meredith). "It's more than an entertainment, it's a panacea," shills Diablo. "You'll shake, you'll shiver, but it's all good fun. The greatest thrill you have ever had in your life!" I suspect that the film was supposed to be called Dr Diabolo's Torture Garden (a la Dr Terror's House of Horrors) and I would have preferred that title because it sounds completely bonkers!

The framing device is ok but not as enjoyable as the ones deployed in the other Amicus films. Peter Cushing's antiques shop in From Beyond the Grave, Robert Powell and Patrick Magee in the asylum, the catacombs in Tales from the Crypt, the swanky basement in Vault of Horror, the train carriage in Dr Terror's House of Horrors. The circus sideshow is rather half-hearted with some rubbish waxworks and Meredith (who was at his best playing ordinary, downtrodden characters in The Twilight Zone) too theatrical and hammy as Diabolo. It is sometimes said that Meredith is basically doing his Penguin from the Batman television show in this film but there is more than a hint of Mr Smith too - Mr Smith being the diabolical and mysterious character he played in the Twilight Zone episode Printer's Devil.

Anyway, Diabolo entices five curious patrons into a backroom where he promises to show them the true meaning of fear. All they have to do is look through the "shears of fate" held by an effigy of the female deity Atropos (Clytie Jessop) - The Goddess Of Destiny. In anthology tradition, we then segue into each segment whenever the characters take him up on this offer and catch a glimpse of what might await them in the future. "The primordial monstrosities that lurk in the mind, to forewarn..."

The first story is called Enoch and serves as a relatively solid beginning to the anthology. Colin Williams (Michael Bryant) is a freeloading playboy with no moral compass who gets wind of the fact that his sick Uncle Roger (Maurice Denham) is close to death and obviously minted because - rumour has it - Roger pays for everything with gold coins. Colin allows his uncle to die by hiding his medicine and then proceeds to look for the gold coins - his trawl taking him to the large cellar. He finds a coffin containing a dead body and a cat that is very much alive. The cat is named Balthazar and Balthazar is no ordinary cat.

Balthazar takes control of Colin's mind and requires nefarious deeds to be undertaken in exchange for the gold coins.

"Your name is Balthazar. You have come to stay with me, to serve me, as you served my uncle. You will reward me as you rewarded him. In return for this there are things I must do for you." If that synopsis sounds a bit silly then I can only remind you that this is an Amicus anthology film and not a documentary about Venezuelan street cleaners. My own cats do nothing but sleep, catch mice, eat Cheese Dreamies, and claw up the armchairs. I suspect that Balthazar would be a lot less expensive to own because he doesn't seem to require any Whiskas or Felix. Still, there are definitely drawbacks to old Balthazar - as this segment will reveal.

This first segment has quite a strong sense of atmospherics with the house suitably eerie and intrigue created by Colin's discovery of the hidden cellar. There are also some grisly deaths - which is fun. Bryant is good too as the increasingly insane central character. The actor had recently performed with the Royal Shakespeare Company and he doesn't play down to the material (always a help in films like this). Look out too for Maurice Denham, an actor who had already enjoyed a long career (including an appearance in the classic British horror film Night of the Demon). Freddie Francis imbues this segment with a good sense of style and the use of light and colour is inventive at times. Enoch is not the most memorable segment in the Amicus anthology hall of fame but it is a reasonably interesting and well staged opening story for Torture Garden. It's a good start to Torture Garden and the rest of the film struggles to keep the momentum going.

The second story is called Terror Over Hollywood and is a fairly maligned entry in the pantheon of omnibus horror films but it does have a Rod Serling's Night Gallery sort of ambiance that is modestly engaging if you can stay interested long enough for the twist. Carla Hayes (Beverly Adams) is a young ambitious actress who sabotages her friend's assignation with a hotshot producer so she can take her place. In the confines of hip nightclub "Danny's", Carla is an embryonic mover and, er, shaker. She meets producer Eddie Storm (John Phillips) and the perpetually youthful leading man Bruce Benton (Robert

Hutton). These Hollywood types seem to be real life Peter Pans and never age or die. What can their secret be?

This is a fairly atypical jaunt for an Amicus segment with the Hollywood setting - albeit one that is less than convincing and was obviously shot in a British studio. Danny's nightclub is hilariously naff with sixties bubble ornaments and some wince inducing hipster dialogue. I did enjoy the twist though even if you do feel like you've seen it before in about a million other films. It's not really the fault of Torture Garden that a particular seventies film essayed this general idea to more famous popular culture effect a decade or so on. To mention the film would be to give the twist away but let's just say that large summer hats and cooking recipes are an important component of that film. Terror Over Hollywood feels a lot more generic than than the (very British) segments in the later Amicus anthology films and is more sci-fi satire than horror. The acting in Terror Over Hollywood is not brilliant and the sets definitely could have been better. Gratuitous trivia: the beautiful Beverly Adams was married to Vidal Sassoon.

The third story is called Mr Steinway and is quite hard to defend for one obvious reason. It revolves around a killer piano. Even by the conventions of the Amicus anthology horror film that's a challenge. How do you tackle this sort of story (and the obvious thing to say would be that you probably shouldn't bother in the first place) without it appearing ludicrous? The answer is you can't and while Mr Steinway is not as bad as legend would have it you couldn't honestly say it was very good either. What is the plot of this bizarre bauble? Journalist Dorothy Endicott (Barbara Ewing) visits the home of shy and reclusive concert pianist Leo (John Standing) to write a piece about him. The pair soon become close and romance blossoms. The problem? Leo's piano seems to be haunted and takes an instant dislike to Dorothy!

This is vaguely reminiscent of a segment in Tales That Witness Madness, a 1973 (non Amicus) British anthology where Joan Collins had to deal with a jealous spooky tree that hated her. I have to say the tree worked better than the piano - although it really shouldn't have done. I'd rather watch the Joan Collins tree segment in Tales That Witness Madness than

Mr Steinway any day of the week. Only in the world of British anthology horror films can you have these weighty debates. Jealous tree versus vengeful piano.

Mr Steinway was the film debut of New Zealand actress Barbara Ewing, later to become a familiar face on British television in her later years. Ewing has a fairly thankless task with her character here but makes the best of it. John Standing (another Amicus star who was respected for his stage work) is pretty good as the shy Norman Bates-ish Leo and at the very least Freddie Francis makes the segment as stylish as he can but Mr Steinway is always fighting a somewhat losing battle. Killer piano indeed.

Torture Garden has been a mixed bag so far and we've endured two fairly forgettable segments on the bounce but we do at least end on a relative high with what is easily the best segment in the film. The Man Who Collected Poe has Jack Palance as an Edgar Allan Poe collector named Ronald Wyatt. Wyatt is more than excited to meet Lancelot Canning (Peter Cushing) as Canning has a very impressive collection of Poe material including the holy grail of a hitherto unpublished manuscript. But Canning's biggest secret awaits for the curious Wyatt to discover....

The Man Who Collected Poe has a fairly decent twist (which somehow manages to survive its inherent daftness) but the real pleasure here comes from the long scene of Cushing and Palance together drinking brandy and discussing Poe. Palance hams it up to the hilt as the drooling Poe obsessive and might as well have a slice of pineapple on his head but both actors palpably seem to be enjoying themselves and acting in this segment together, making the most of every line or word that comes their way. Cushing is much more restrained and - as ever - fulfils his regular role of thoroughly classing up the film he is in.

If the other stories in Torture Garden had been this watchable then I think this anthology would be much more fondly remembered than it is. The only shame with this story is that Christopher Lee might well have had the Palance role were it not for the fact that, as we have already mentioned, for reasons of financing the film, some name recognition

American guest stars (i.e, Meredith and Palance) were shunted in. The Man Who Collected Poe would have been even more enjoyable with Cushing and Lee together again. At the very least, The Man Who Collected Poe does enable Torture Garden to end on a relative high. This is certainly a patchy anthology film though with weak middle sections. The general atmosphere lacks the cosy Britishness of Dr Terror's House and Horrors to the point where it sometimes feels more we are watching an American anthology show of the era like Night Gallery.

We then of course return to Diabolo and his patrons for a somewhat predictable wraparound wrapup. Torture Garden is by no means a bad film and you'll have a good time with a couple of the stories but it does feel like the least essential of the Amicus portmanteau films and doesn't have the kitsch fun rewatch factor of the anthology films they produced in the early seventies. The first and last stories are above average but the framing scenes and the two middle stories are nothing to write home about and drag the film down a few notches from where it potentially could have been. For me anyway, Torture Garden is the least fun of the Amicus anthology films to watch.

* The Twilight Zone ran from 1959 for 156 episodes and remains an enduringly iconic part of American television history. It was created by Rod Serling - who also wrote many of the episodes and always appeared near the start to present an introduction monologue to camera ("Submitted for your perusal...") and then ended each episode with a closing piece of narration in his distinctive manner and voice. The series was alternately spine chilling and poignant as each week a variety of characters took a wrong turn into the Twilight Zone, a place where anything could and often did happen. In addition to Serling, the series had many episodes written by talented people like Charles Beaumont, Richard Matheson and Earl Hamner Jr and a host of actors who would become familiar names were on the show. Robert Redford, Burt Reynolds, William Shatner, Charles Bronson, Elizabeth Montgomery and so on. The series even had a sort of regular company of actors who would frequently appear in different

episodes. Perhaps the two most cherished Twilight Zone stalwarts were Burgess Meredith and Jack Klugman. You know an episode is going to be good if Meredith or Klugman are in it. Well, apart from Mr Dingle, the Strong obviously.

DANGER ROUTE (1967)

Danger Route was directed by Seth Holt and written by Meade Roberts and Robert Banks Stewart. It was based on Andrew York's 1966 novel The Eliminator. Seth Holt was an editor and producer on many great films - like The Ladykillers, Saturday Night and Sunday Morning, The Lavender Hill Mob. He also directed Bette Davis in The Nanny and was a director on the popular Patrick McGoohan television show Danger Man. Holt tragically died of a heart attack while directing the 1971 Hammer film Blood from the Mummy's Tomb. He was only 47.

Although Amicus Productions was a horror studio they would occasionally try something out of their usual comfort zone. One such film was Danger Route, an espionage thriller made at the back end of the sixties spy craze. This film features Richard Johnson as British spy Jonas Wilde. This was clearly an attempt by Amicus to hitch their wagon to the Bondmania of the 1960s - which was more or less at or just past its apex at this point (adjusted for inflation, 1965's Thunderball is the biggest grossing James Bond film of all time). Milton Subotsky didn't like Danger Route very much and felt they missed the boat by making it at the tail end of the sixties spy cycle.

Anyone expecting a James Bond pastiche or copycat will probably be disappointed by Danger Route. Danger Route takes itself far more seriously than the 1960s Bond films and doesn't have much money or spectacle at its disposal. Jonas wants to retire in the film but is told he can only resign if he does one last mission. This mission involves killing a Czech defector who is in the custody of the Americans. Jonas manages to complete his mission but then becomes aware that his superior has vanished and British agents are being murdered. There seems to be a traitor or some sort of double-cross at play. Jonas resolves to get the bottom of this knotty espionage mystery.

This is a strange sort of film that positions itself somewhere in the gulf between the high fantasy Bond films and more down to earth and gritty Harry Palmer series with Michael Caine. The Harry Palmer films were a very stylish sixties antidote or counterpoint to the fantastical and glossy James Bond series. It was ironically Bond producer Harry Saltzman who decided to use Deighton's novels as the source for a very different type of cinematic spy series.

Whereas Sean Connery's agent was lavishly equipped with ingenious gadgets, visited numerous exotic sun-drenched locales, frequently wore a tuxedo and saved the world on a regular basis in a total fantasy environment with absolute loyalty to Queen and Country, Harry Palmer was a downbeat, cynical, anti-authoritarian spy who wore thick NHS specs, shopped in supermarkets and munched on cornflakes. It was a clever move to go in a radically different direction by Saltzman and subsequently the Palmer series exists on its own terms as an intelligent and interesting series of films rather than leave itself too open to the charge of being a Bond clone in an era that was festooned with them.

James Bond is a playboy of sorts, an urbane expense account snob and former Royal Navy Commander who had a private education. Harry Palmer on the other hand is an ordinary Joe, working off a two-year sentence for black market activities he undertook in Berlin once. You'd say that Danger Route is much closer to Harry Palmer than it is to the likes of Goldfinger and Thunderball. Jonas Wilde is quite a downbeat character and clearly has no particular love for his occupation or the people he works for.

When we meet Jonas in the film he seems as if he wants nothing more than to walk away from the world of spying and espionage and put it all behind him. This aspect to the character and the melancholic jazzy score feels very Harry Palmer. Danger Route occasionally veers into Bond territory when Jonas seduces or charms women and karate chops people during fights. Jonas can kill with a single karate chop -

and frequently does!

Other would be Bonds of the sixties included Matt Helm and Derek Flint. Helm starred in thirty novels by Donald Hamilton and the government operative got to the big screen when Columbia pictures decided to jump onto the Bond craze. In a move that probably didn't please all Helm fans, the pictures were spoofs with a slightly sozzled looking Dean Martin lending his laid-back style to proceedings. The Silencers (1966), Murderer's Row (1966), The Ambushers (1967), and The Wrecking Crew (1968) are sporadically entertaining but laissez faire with the source material.

Our Man Flint, a 1966 film directed by Daniel Mann attempted to create a character who could beat Bond at his own game. Tongue-in-cheek and witty, Derek Flint, like 007 armed with a neverending array of arcane knowledge, battled nefarious world threatening organisations with exotic gadgetry while finding time for numerous beautiful women. James Coburn brought his toothy charisma to the part. The film was well received but 1967's In Like Flint seemed to stretch the joke a bit too far. Derek Flint was more or less done although he, perhaps as much as Bond, inspired Mike Myers one-joke Austin Powers series. Ray Danton later played Flint in a 1976 television pilot.

Richard Johnson featured in much more obviously James Bondish films than Danger Route around this time as Bulldog Drummond in Deadlier Than the Male and Some Girls Do. The strange irony of Johnson's numerous sixties spy roles lay in the fact that he was the first choice of the Bond producers and director Terence Young to play James Bond in Dr No but turned down their offer because he didn't want to sign what he saw as a constrictive long term contract to one studio. That paved the way for Sean Connery to take the part of 007. If he'd so desired though, Richard Johnson could have been the first cinema James Bond.

To be fair to Richard Johnson he obviously had no idea that the Bond films were going to be so successful! He gave an interview once where he made some interesting observations about turning down James Bond. Johnson said that Sean Connery was completely wrong for the part of Bond as depicted in the books by Ian Fleming but completely RIGHT for the cinematic version of Bond created by Terence Young, Broccoli and Saltzman. Richard Johnson felt that he could have played the Bond from the books but he couldn't have brought the tongue-in-cheek humour and macho sex appeal to the cinematic Bond in the way that Connery did - and it was these very qualities which propelled it to success.

Johnson is a pretty good leading man in Danger Route. He's handsome and suave but quite sarcastic. Jonas Wilde feels much more like a real person than James Bond and Richard Johnson gives him a believable inner life of regret and frustration. There's quite a good section of the film where Jonas poses as a brush salesmen (!) to seduce a housekeeper played by Diana Dors so he can get close to his target in a big house.

Richard Johnson has to affect a more 'common' accent for this ruse and it might have come off as risible and preposterous in lesser hands but the actor sort of makes it work. It's great to see Diana Dors here in a part that captures her mid-phase so to speak. She's no longer Britain's version of Marilyn Monroe and yet to adopt those battleaxe wife or sinister grandmother parts she would end up playing in the seventies. Here she is somewhere in the middle trying to work out where her career is going. By the way, watch a film called Yield to the Night to see what a great actress Diana Dors could be.

Carol Lynley plays the beautiful and mysterious young woman that Jonas falls for. Lynley is here to add some glamour to the film and her scenes have a glitz and soft-focus fantasy aura in contrast to the rest of Danger Route. The scenes of Johnson and Lynley together in some swanky flat are the closest Danger Route comes to feeling like a Bond film. Sylvia Syms also has a rather mysterious part as Barbara Canning although she doesn't get that much to do in the film. We keep going and back and forth in the story to Johnson on a boat with Gordon Jackson, who plays some sort of contact. These scenes have some rather obvious back projection which looks terribly amateurish.

I gather that Danger Route was a troubled production and

they had to change the main cameraman at some point. Milton Subotsky didn't have anything nice to say about Danger Route and seemed to feel it was one of the worst films that Amicus made. I think that's probably a trifle harsh but some of the production issues are detectable when you watch the film. Amicus were never exactly awash with money and all of this, plus the director apparently falling ill, might account for a few scenes that seem to lack the reasonably competent nature of the rest of Danger Route. There's a strange scene where Johnson and Dors are in a house when - all of a sudden - they seem to be surrounded by fake plants and acting with just a wall behind them. Maybe this was a scene they added later?

Unusually for a spy film, our hero never actually travels abroad in the story (although we gather that Jonas has just returned from the West Indies). Much of the story seems to take place in the Channel Islands. There's no big set-piece or climax to the film. The only action you get is when Jonas deploys his faithful karate chop. There's quite a good fight in a corridor though that wouldn't have shamed a sixties Bond film. It reminded me slightly of a punch-up George Lazenby has in a corridor in On Her Majesty's Secret Service. The story in Danger Route is a little confusing at times although you'll probably be able to guess who the traitor is long before we reach the end. I suspect this film might be far too slow and uneventful for some tastes but Danger Route is not bad at all really - thanks mostly to the strong performance of Richard Johnson. It's no Harry Palmer film but Danger Route is a mildly interesting relic from the dusty vaults of Amicus Productions.

A TOUCH OF LOVE (1969)

A Touch of Love was directed by Waris Hussein and adapted by Margaret Drabble from her novel The Millstone. Waris Hussein directed the early episodes of Doctor Who. He also directed one of my favourite British films of the 1970s - Melody. A Touch of Love is a very atypical Amicus film. They obviously thought they'd try their hand at something completely different and the end result is this talky drama. It was an experiment that Amicus never repeated - although around this time Max Rosenberg and Milton Subotsky did produce a film version of Harold Pinter's The Birthday Party for another studio.

I suppose Amicus making a film like this was like when Cannon Films were churning out Chuck Norris actioners and films about breakdancing and ninjas (I'm surprised they didn't combine the two - Breakdancing Ninja!) but would still occasionally do something more serious like War and Love, Salomè, Barfly, Powaqqatsi and Runaway Train. It's like when a comedian does a straight dramatic role in a film. They just want to prove there is more than one string to their bow.

A Touch of Love never really found an audience and these days you'd be hard pressed to find anyone who is even aware of this film's existence. This is one of those films that I don't recall ever encountering on television. Milton Subotsky liked A Touch of Love and according to his wife it was one of his favourite Amicus films. A Touch of Love was called Thank You All Very Much in the United States. You'd have thought just calling it The Millstone like the novel would have been a better idea than these other titles but presumably they decided The Millstone wasn't a very catchy or commercial film title - which is fair enough I suppose. The Millstone does sound a bit like a period drama about bread baking or something.

Anyway, the story in A Touch of Love revolves around Rosamund (Sandy Dennis), an independent minded young woman studying for a doctorate in London. She spends a lot of time in the British library. However, after a drunken fumble with journalist George (a young Ian McKellen) she falls pregnant and must cope with the trials of single motherhood. Rosamund's main solace and support in this drama comes from her eccentric friend Lydia (Eleanor Bron). A Touch of Love is far from the best drama British cinema produced in the sixties. This is no A Taste of Honey or Saturday Night, Sunday Morning. The film though is not a complete a waste of time but it does become something of an ordeal in the end at just over one hour and forty minutes.

The lead actress here is Sandy Dennis - who you'll definitely recognise. I know her from (later) films like Alan Alda's The Four Seasons and Woody Allen's Another Woman. I also know her from the eighties horror film 976-EVIL but I doubt that Sandy would want to be remembered for that one too much. Sandy Dennis was American but she's quite convincing in A Touch of Love with an English accent and brings an understated wryness and intelligence to the part. If I had a criticism it would be that her performance as Rosamund is very controlled. In the film you have all these men taking an interest in her as if Rosamund is very magnetic and charismatic but she's not exactly a barrel of laughs.

Sandy Dennis also seems a bit old for this part. There is actually a flashback scene at one point where you have her in school uniform to depict Rosamund coming home from school. Sandy Dennis was in her thirties when they made this film so she's a bit long in the tooth to be playing a schoolgirl. Eleanor Bron is really the main support in A Touch of Love and her comic timing manages to float the film through a few lulls. She works well with Sandy Dennis. Bron was part of the comic satire boom of the 1960s and her charisma is much needed in a Touch of Love. Eleanor Bron actually reminds me quite a bit of Phoebe Waller-Bridge in this film.

The story concerns Rosamund becoming pregnant but then having to decide whether or not to have the baby and also whether or not to tell her friends and the ACTUAL father who the father of the baby is. I gather that this screen adaptation is very faithful to the book. Rosamund then has to cope with the difficulties of having a child when you are a single mother. This is not a kitchen sink social realism film at all though. The characters are all novelists, or newsreaders, or studying, and all have nice flats. There are party scenes and restaurant scenes and everyone drinks gin and talks like a character in a play rather than a real person. I can't say I related to anyone in this film very much.

One of the strangest parts of the film comes with the treatment of Rosamund in hospital. They seem desperate to make her put her baby up for adoption. Were hospitals really so cold and prejudiced when it came to single mothers in the sixties? Perhaps they were. I really don't know but the depiction of the NHS is far from flattering. I haven't read The Millstone but presumably Margaret Drabble had criticisms of the health service from personal experience which she wanted to lace into the story. It's rather weird to see a young Ian McKellen with a mop of black hair in this film. He's quite good in A Touch of Love (if giving a very mannered performance which seems more suited to the stage) although he doesn't feature as much as you might expect.

There's some nice location work in A Touch of Love * and I enjoyed the London streets, cars, and parks of the late 1960s. The scene in the British Library was shot on a Sunday and cost Amicus £6,000 because they had to rig lights and get a crew in there. One thing I liked about the film too is that at the party scenes you see some black guests. A Touch of Love acknowledges the fact that London was a very multi-cultural city by now. There's a good cast in this film on the whole with the likes of Michael Coles and also John Standing (an Amicus stalwart by now) popping up. I was very impressed by the way that John Standing has a restaurant scene with Sandy Denis and while she's merely picking at her food he's shoveling the grub down like there's no tomorrow. Eating and acting is not easy but John Standing proves to be an expert!

A Touch of Love is competent but a very flat and unengaging sort of film. This is the sort of film that you can barely remember anything about afterwards. I don't think there is any good reason to track down A Touch of Love but if you are an Amicus completist you might want to give it a go. I doubt it would be a film you'll be in a rush to return to again though. I like Sandy Dennis and Eleanor Bron but even these two talented actors struggle to breathe much life into this forgettable drama. And at one hour and forty seven minutes, A Touch of Love unavoidably outstays its welcome in the end. This film wasn't hugely successful and Amicus never attempted to make anything like it again. It would be back to horror, thrillers, and sci-fi for Amicus from here on in.

* There is some fascinatingly bizarre trivia about this film on IMDB. It says that the footage of the Post Office Tower in the

film was contrary to regulations because at the time you weren't allowed to show the tower in films due to its strategic communications importance. It was supposed to be a secret building and didn't even feature on maps. How could one possibly expect to keep the Post Officer Tower secret? You can see it for miles!

SCREAM AND SCREAM AGAIN (1970)

Scream and Scream Again was directed by Gordon Hessler and written by Christopher Wicking. Michael Reeves (of Witchfinder General fame) was supposed to direct this film but he sadly died only weeks before production was due to begin. It is based on the novel The Disorientated Man by Peter Saxon (a pseudonym used by various authors in the 1960). In the book aliens were the villains but they got rid of that in this film so you won't find any alien shenanigans here.

I suspect that after the Doctor Who films, The Terrornauts, and They Came From Beyond Space, Amicus were a trifle weary of sci-fi films and didn't want to make another one in a hurry. Gordon Hessler (who had worked with Vincent Price on The Oblong Box) said he got screenwriter Christopher Wicking to rework the script because the one Milton Subotsky wrote wasn't really filmable. Subotsky seemed to be a bit irritated by this because he never spoke too fondly about Scream and Scream Again.

Scream and Scream Again is - famously - absolutely bonkers. This is more of a surreal thriller than a horror film despite the wonderfully melodramatic (and very Amicus) pulp title. The film uses a non-linear narrative and intricate plot twists to keep the audience engaged. It explores themes of science gone wrong and government conspiracy. Scream and Scream Again got mixed reviews when it came out but these days is regarded to be something of a mild cult classic. Vincent Price once said in an interview that he couldn't make head nor tail of Scream and Scream Again and had no idea what the film was supposed to be.

You, the viewer, will share that experience but you know what? I think that's actually the point of this film. This film is as mad as a hatter and all over the place and you'll either enjoy that quality or be frustrated by it. It all begins with a jogger ambling through London as the titles roll. The jogger has what appears to be a heart attack and wakes up in a private hospital room where he's being attended to by a nurse who doesn't talk much. Doesn't sound too bad I suppose. All except for one thing. Each time he wakes up he seems to be missing another limb! What on earth is going on?

Meanwhile, in an unknown Eastern European country, where some sort of fascist government seems to be in power, intelligence operative Konartz (Marshall Jones) is given a briefing by his superior, who is no lesser figure than Cleggy from Last of the Summer Wine (aka actor Peter Sallis). Konartz promptly gives Cleggy a Vulcan neck pinch, killing him almost instantly. And as far as the plot threads in Scream and Scream Again go, last, but by no means least, we have a killer on the loose in London. The killer seems to be a shaggy haired Michael Gothard in a purple shirt. The sarcastic Police Superintendent Bellaver (Alfred Marks) is assigned to the case.

Scream and Scream Again is a tremendously confusing film the first time you watch it. You have all these different plot threads all jumbled together and none of them seem to make any sense. Really though, that turns out to be the main charm of the film - the outrageously eccentric 'throw the kitchen sink' at the story approach to it all. To be fair, they do tie everything together at the end and while it still doesn't make sense at least they tried!

The presence of horror icons Christopher Lee, Peter Cushing, and Vincent Price in the same film is (sadly) somewhat misleading. All have minor roles and Cushing vanishes after one scene where he plays a leader in the totalitarian state and gets a Vulcan death pinch from Konartz. Cushing was only hired for one day by Amicus - which explains why he's not in the film much. Vincent Price appears a few times as a mad doctor named Dr Browning experimenting in transplants, and Christopher Lee plays a small part as a snooty and mysterious intelligence bigwig named Fremont.

The only time any of them share a scene is at the end when Lee and Price appear together but it doesn't last for very long and you barely see them in the same frame. It's a shame really that none of these legends appear for longer or share any notable scenes. I think this is why some people are disappointed when they watch this film and partly explains why it has such a low rating on IMDB. You see the names Price, Cushing, and Lee but when you watch the film they barely interact and don't feature very much.

Much of the screen time then rests on Alfred Marks as the no nonsense Superintendent Bellaver. Marks (who apparently improvised his dialogue) is quite funny and droll in the film. He's rather like Donald Pleasance in the (later) British horror film Death Line - though not as much fun because it is impossible for anyone to top the comic performance by Pleasance in Death Line. Interestingly, Christopher Lee also played a mysterious and snooty intelligence/government bigwig in Death Line too. He's essentially playing the same character here in Scream and Scream Again that he played in Death Line.

Scream and Scream Again mitigates the haphazard nature of the plot with plenty of action and an upbeat poppy music score. There's a long sequence where Michael Gothard is chased by the police (for what seems like forever) that is really well directed. There's none of the terrible back projection you usually get in films of this era when they have car chase sequences. This is a tyre screeching car chase on a real road. It's great fun. Parts of the chase were filmed at the Alpine Circuit at Millbrook test track - which was later used for the 'motorcycle skull rider' sequence in Tales from the Crypt.

The police keep getting duffed up by Gothard too when they try to apprehend him as he's supposed to be superhuman. I must say though, the police don't show too much evidence of street smarts when they handcuff him to a car and then wander off to have a chat. If someone had just beaten up a dozen coppers and displayed superhuman strength I'd probably want to keep a closer eye on him!

The third act finds Scream and Scream Again shifting into another gear and has Christopher Matthews as Dr David Sorel becoming the main character as he seeks to understand what exactly is going on - a desire greatly shared by the audience! It feels like there are three or four separate films in Scream and Scream Again all jostling together and fighting one another for space. It all swings back to Vincent Price in the last act as the mad doctor. If someone HAS to explain the plot and give a grand speech at the end of Scream and Scream Again, then I can think of no one better than Vincent Price to perform this duty!

Scream and Scream Again is a really bizarre film that is difficult to describe. It doesn't make an awful lot of sense and the various plot strands in the first half don't even seem to belong in the same film let alone mesh together but somehow, miraculously, it all sort of works in the end. Scream and Scream Again has grown in stature over the years and even become something of a cult film. There has never been anything quite like it before or since, this strange blending of different story arcs, genres, and characters.

One minute you've got Peter Cushing in what looks like an SS uniform and then we're at a London disco or something. You never know what to expect next in Scream and Scream Again and that's the secret of its charm and entertainment factor. There's a fine cast, plenty of action, good direction, some shocks, twists and turns, and a general aura of surreal insanity and unpredictability that quickly makes you want to stop nitpicking and just surrender yourself to the enjoyable madness that is Scream and Scream Again.

Scream and Scream Again is not going to be everyone's cup of tea. I find this film highly entertaining myself but others may find the lack of coherence a weakness rather than a strength. The film seems a bit darker and more grisly than the usual fare served up by Amicus and does at least serve to illustrate that the studio were prepared to try different things and weren't just giving you the same film over and over again. This film is difficult to place into any one specific category and is a sort of dark action conspiracy thriller with elements of horror. You may or may not fall for the doolally crazy charms of Scream and Scream Again but you won't be able to deny that this is a unique experience quite unlike anything dished up by Amicus - or anyone else for that matter!

THE MIND OF MR SOAMES (1970)

The Mind of Mr Soames was directed by Alan Cooke and written by John Hale and Edward Simpson. Alan Cooke was a prolific director who spent most of his career in television. He directed episodes on shows like Airwolf, Matlock, Lou Grant, Quincy M.E, Hart to Hart, Murder She Wrote and many others. He also directed the Paint Me a Murder episode of Hammer House of Mystery & Suspense. It is impossible to credit The Mind of Mr Soames to any one writer. Milton Subosky said this film's script was rewritten 20 times and that numerous people had a bash at it. The film is based on Charles Eric Maine's 1961 novel of the same name. This isn't really a horror film (although one might venture that the plot owes something to Frankenstein). It's more of a drama with a few sprinklings of science fiction.

The film concerns a Mr John Soames (Terence Stamp). Soames has been in a coma since birth and is now thirty years-old. A brilliant surgeon named Dr Michael Bergen (Robert Vaughn) finally revives him amidst great publicity. Soames is now essentially a thirty year-old infant. He must learn to walk, eat, and communicate. However a battle ensues between Bergen and the head of this medical institution, Dr Maitland (Nigel Davenport), over how Soames should be treated. Maitland favours a tough love regime whereas Bergen wants to respect Soames as a human being and feels that Maitland is more interested in the medical 'experiment' than the welfare of Soames.

The Mind of Mr Soames is a rather strange film that is difficult to describe. The premise is not a million miles away from the Robin Williams film Awakenings. Interestingly, the start of the film is slightly reminiscent of The Truman Show. We see that a camera crew is there to record the revival of Soames and they also chart his progress as he is treated and taught how to speak and eat. One could say that this film is somewhat ahead of its time in anticipating the future tidal wave of reality television and fly on the wall documentaries. I wouldn't have minded a bit more focus on this aspect of the film - the television crew that is covering this remarkable patient. The story concerns themes of identity, consciousness, and personal freedom.

The Mind of Mr Soames is rather downbeat film and a lot rests on the performance of Stamp. Having to play a fully grown man who is like an infant or child is definitely skating on thin ice when it comes to acting. This could easily have been a risible film if Stamp wasn't good and although it skates close to unintentional comedy a few times when Stamp learns to eat and throws a few tantrums early on, his performance gets better and better as the film goes on - especially when Soames picks up the basics of human behaviour and escapes from the institution. He is a hopeless innocent though and if The Mind of Dr Soames has a message it is that innocence as a commodity is not valued very highly in the cynical world we live in.

The best scenes in the film come when Soames wanders the gardens of the institution, captivated by the plants and nature around him. He sticks his head in a pond to look at a frog and is thrilled by this glimpse of the world beyond his room. There's a wonderful shot of mist shrouded lawns here. I love also the scene where Soames enters a pub and helps himself to a sandwich. He doesn't understand that you have to pay for things with money and can't just help yourself to anything. When he is given a pint of ale he spits it out as he was expecting it to taste like milk.

There's rather a good scene too where Soames is on a train and starts talking to the young woman sharing his compartment. He asks what her name is and starts talking about how many trees there are near his room. She just thinks he's a weirdo and promptly pulls the alarm. Soames has clearly not learnt yet an important rule in British society. You must never start talking to complete strangers on public transport because they'll take you for a nutter!

Robert Vaughn has probably never been better than he is in The Mind of Mr Soames. He isn't playing a hero or a dashing spy. He's doing some proper acting for a change as the kind hearted Dr Bergen. It's nice to see Vaughn playing a more human and vulnerable sort of character. Vaughn more than holds his own with the excellent Nigel Davenport as Maitland. Maitland is - shrewdly - not an out and out villain. He just has different methods and a lot of self-belief. Maitland has run this institution for some time and in the end doesn't take too kindly to Bergen coming in and questioning his theories. Nigel Davenport was in many things but I always remember him the most for the weird but compelling Phase IV. *

The relationship between Bergen and Maitland is well handled in The Mind of Dr Soames though. They are mostly respectful of one another and even seem to get on quite well at the start. When the friction arrives it feels like it is conveyed and developed in a believable way. There's a great cast here - which also includes Donal Donnelly and Norman Jones. The Mind of Mr Soames is a strange film and quite grim in places but it's always a reasonably interesting one with a few inventive flourishes. It's the cast that really make this worth watching. Stamp, Vaughn and Davenport all give performances that deserve to be seen. Look fast by the way too for Christopher Timothy (of All Creatures Great and Small fame) as a camera operator near the start.

This is a fairly unique film in the history of Amicus in the way that it's a straight drama but with sci-fi trappings. Despite their reputation as the 'other British horror studio', Amicus could be quite bold and surprising at times with their films. They certainly weren't afraid to take a few risks. While not everything they tried worked, even the films that never quite hit the mark or found an audience were often interesting. That is certainly the case with The Mind of Mr Soames. This remains a little known film but it is worth watching. The Mind of Mr Soames is not without flaws though and not what you would describe as some obscure lost classic. A salient problem with this film is that it never quite solves the main problem posed by the story. What do you do with Soames once he leaves the institution? The film becomes more uneven when this happens though it does, as we've mentioned, have its moments.

The Mind of Mr Soames is what you could arguably describe as a high concept film. The notion of a thirty year-old who had the mind of an infant and so must learn everything from scratch is interesting but whether or not the screenplay does justice to that concept and manages to make the concept work for an entire film is certainly open to question. I quite like this film and the cast are great but I don't think The Mind of Mr Soames is something that you'd find yourself returning to very much when it comes to the Amicus back catalogue. This is one of those films that you watch, find quite interesting, but then sort of forget about. It isn't something which you would be drawn back to purely for entertainment or escapism. It isn't really that sort of film. Amicus would return to horror after The Mind of Mr Soames as the next anthology film was waiting in the wings.

* The 1973 film Phase IV was directed by Saul Bass - best known for designing title sequences for classic films like Psycho. Phase IV is a truly strange film but a very unique experience. The film is set in the desert where a couple of scientists (played by Nigel Davenport and Michael Murphy) living in a sealed bio dome end up matching wits against a species of ants which has gained super intelligence. The film is every bit as weird as that synopsis makes it sound but novel for a number of reasons. For one the ants are normal sized. These ants are not lumbering monsters like something out of 1950s science fiction but crafty little critters who - by the end of the film - have gained intelligence way beyond that of man. Welcome to our new insect overlords.

Phase IV has some incredible insect photography that makes it a truly surreal experience at times. What is remarkable about the film is how it gives us the perspective of the ants as much as it does the humans. They truly become equal characters in the story. Phase IV seems obsessed with geometric shapes and patterns and makes us ponder the incredible ability of ants to build and work as a society. In many ways ants and humans are strangely similar. Both species assign roles, both build and work together, and both can be destructive and cruel. It's quite trippy when the ant language is represented by strange waves on a computer screen. The story makes us question the arrogance of man when it comes to respecting other life on the planet - however small. Phase IV is not for all tastes but a very singular and trippy experience all the same. Make sure you don't miss out on watching that amazing full deleted (very psychedelic) ending.

THE HOUSE THAT DRIPPED BLOOD (1970)

The third in the Amicus anthology series, The House That Dripped Blood was allocated a budget of £500,000 and again was based at Shepperton studios. Peter Duffell replaced Freddie Francis in the director's chair as Francis apparently had a fractious relationship with Subotsky on the last compendium and was unavailable at the time anyway. This was the first film credit for Duffell (he'd directed a lot on television including episodes of The Avengers and Man in a Suitcase). Milton Subotsky chose Duffell and later gave Kevin Connor a similar chance to make his name with Amicus.

"How did I get it? Well, I was offered it!" said Duffell. "Milton Subotsky, the producer, was quite happy to employ young directors without any big track record; to give them the chance, as it were. And I think Milton had seen some of my television work and he offered me the job. So there we were. I wasn't going to turn it down! At that time, there was very little being made in the British film industry except horror movies. It was one way in." Duffell wanted to call the film Death and the Maiden but obviously didn't get his way in the end. Milton Subotsky and Max Rosenberg, as one can see from the Amicus catalogue, loved lurid film titles because they attracted more attention and looked great on the poster. Death and the Maiden is a classier title than The House That Dripped Blood but it isn't nearly as much fun.

Max Rosenberg said The House That Dripped Blood was a title he had come up with ages ago for no particular reason. He was happy to finally have a film to slap it on! According to Peter Duffell, Peter Cushing and Christopher Lee also agreed with him that The House That Dripped Blood was a "lousy" title. Max Rosenberg said he spent an entire year reading Robert Bloch stories before he chose the ones for The House That Dripped Blood. Milton Subotsky would also endlessly read horror stories and scripts looking for things that might be suitable for an Amicus film. Milton estimated that he read about 500 books a year!

"I did try in the film to get a different look to each of the four stories," said Duffell of his approach to The House That Dripped Blood. "In terms of the sets, we used different parts of the house to focus on in each story – although the characters walked through each room – but the centre of each story was in a different room. In that way, I tried to avoid the monotony of the individual backgrounds; so no-one was always looking at the same sofa or bookcase, or what ever."

Vincent Price was offered the part of horror film actor Paul Henderson but had to decline because of a contract with American International Pictures. He was replaced by Jon Pertwee, an actor who had just become the third incarnation of Doctor Who on television. Gratuitous trivia - Pertwee got the part of Doctor Who because Ron Moody turned it down.

Pertwee said he based his horror actor character in The House That Dripped Blood on Christopher Lee but Lee didn't even notice that he was being spoofed! Hammer icon Ingrid Pitt also joined the cast. Peter Cushing returned again although his wife Helen was unwell at he time and he understandably would have preferred not to do the film. Sadly, Helen died in 1971.

The House That Dripped Blood was shot in just under a month and wrapped on the 28th of July 1970. The screenplay is credited to Robert Bloch and Russ Jones (best known as the creator of the magazine Creepy for Warren Publishing). The exteriors of two different houses were used for the titular house in this film. One building was in the grounds of Shepperton Studios and the other was quite close (this would be in Surrey obviously) to the studio. The real location for the wax museum in the second segment is Weybridge Hall in Weybridge. This building is on the corner of Church Street and Minorca Road. Michael Dress provided a memorable score for The House That Dripped Blood. He had also scored A Touch of Love and The Mind of Mr Soames for Amicus. Sadly, Michael Dress died in 1975 at the young age of 39.

We get four stories in The House That Dripped Blood - all set in and around the same spooky Home Counties country house and as ever with Amicus there is a framing device spun around the various tales with Inspector Holloway (John Bennett) of Scotland Yard being asked to investigate the mysterious disappearance of the last tenant of this infamous and apparently haunted property - faded horror film star Paul Henderson (Jon Pertwee). Inspector Holloway is duly told about the troubled history of the house at the police station in the framing scenes as we see the evidence for ourselves in the four stories. This isn't the greatest framing sequence as far as Amicus anthology films go but it isn't bad and does have a nice (creepy) coda.

The first story is called Method For Murder and has horror novelist Charles Hillyer (Denholm Elliott) moving into the spooky house with wife Alice (Joanna Dunham) to work on his latest book in (he hopes) peace and quiet. Hillyer however becomes increasingly unsettled by the eerie nature of the house and visions of the murderous protagonist of his latest hack offering, a homicidal strangler called Dominic (Tom Adams). Dominic is soon making more and more eerie cameo appearances in the murky shadows of the house as Hillyer's sanity and nerves come under increasing strain. Is he going mad or is the fictional Dominic really haunting him?

Method For Murder is a very watchable and fairly intriguing opening tale for The House That Dripped Blood and although it is incredibly simple in its construction and story it generates a good deal of eeriness and atmosphere as Hillyer begins to see his fictional killer in the house late at night more and more.

The blurring of the line between fantasy and reality and frazzled state of mind of a man who might be losing his grip on sanity is all conveyed in competent fashion. Director Peter Duffell does a good job in presenting us and Hillyer with little glimpses of Dominic in the gloom and shadows and there is a fairly decent twist at the end which you may or may not have seen coming.

There is a good cast in this first segment besides Denholm Elliott. Robert Lang turns up as a doctor and Joanna Dunham, an acclaimed stage actor who had been in films like The Greatest Story Ever Told, is also good as Mrs Hillyer. Tom Adams, who looked like the Milk-Tray Man in real life and played secret agent Charles Vine in a series of James Bond comedy knock-offs around this time, is also effective as the man in Hillyer's paranoid visions.

This opening segment segment eschews some of the camp we associate with Amicus and so comes across as agreeably straight faced and taut. A major plus of course is the presence of the always dependable Denholm Elliott - who is wonderfully twitchy as Hillyer starts to come under ever more strain. The old house of the film's title has a rather anachronistic and creaky quality too which helps this segment a great deal. Method For Murder is a solid start to the anthology and is probably the scariest and creepiest of the tales on offer in The House That Dripped Blood.

The second story is called Waxworks and stars the legendary Peter Cushing as Philip Grayson, a rather solitary bachelor who moves into the house with his collection of highly memorable cardigans. Grayson wants a nice quiet life now for some mysterious reason connected to the dim and distant past and we see him listening to his classical music records in the house and generally pottering about keeping himself to himself on strolls through the town. Unfortunately though he just happens to pass by a rather tatty waxworks - Jacquelin's Museum of Horror - in the high street and becomes oddly entranced by a waxwork of Salome bearing the head of John the Baptist.

This waxworks triggers a very bittersweet memory for Grayson and is the device which sets the story in motion. The arrival of Phillip's friend Neville Rogers, played by the excellent Joss Ackland in one of the campest and largest neck scarves in cinematic history, duly complicates matters when he too becomes obsessed with Salome and can't stay away from the waxworks. Why does this waxwork have such power over these two men?

Waxworks is a story I have a weakness for in The House That Dripped Blood just for the presence alone of Peter Cushing in some of the largest collars and most extraordinary cravats imaginable. As usual Cushing gives a wonderfully committed and sympathetic performance as Grayson, a man haunted by an enigmatic past event and looking for some peace and seclusion. Peter Duffell says that he actually made some changes to the script to tailor it more for Cushing. "I did change it. I introduced some scenes. I never met Bloch, although Milton Subotsky knew him well, of course. He'd done other stories for him. But for my film, I think that Bloch was unhappy with my treatment of the Wax Museum story with Peter Cushing. I'm only told this you know. He was unhappy with it because it shifted the balance of the story from the mad axe murderer who ran the wax museum, to the character played by Cushing. But then Cushing was the star, so it played better that way."

The arrival of Joss Ackland in Waxworks merely adds to the fun and the mystery starts to make sense when we discover the link between the two men - conveyed in a touching line from Ackland. Wolfe Morris is also enjoyable as the nutty owner of Jacquelin's Museum of Horror, a place that is quite good fun when the characters visit after being drawn to the place by a particular attraction. Waxworks ultimately becomes rather silly but this segment is always interesting and the presence of Cushing and Ackland lifts everything up a few notches and makes it all the more watchable.

The third story is called Sweets To The Sweet and stars Christopher Lee as John Reed, a rather stern and unemotional man who moves into the house with his young daughter Jane (Chloe Franks). Jane's new home tutor Ann Norton (Nyree Dawn Porter) however finds herself increasingly troubled by the strict martinet Reed's cold refusal to let Jane go to school, see other children, or even have toys. There is perhaps a strange method to this madness though as Reed suggests when he talks about his late wife. "I was glad when she died," he says mysteriously. "Because by then I had found out... " Found out what? What is the secret behind his strange behaviour?

Sweets To The Sweet is not the best story here but a decent addition to the anthology and although it builds to a somewhat predictable ending (you'll surely know what the pay-off will be a long time before we actually arrive at this point or the revelations and clues come) there is much to enjoy here, most notably the performance of Christopher Lee - who is at his snotty, sneering best as the strict father who seems to be incredibly wary of and cold with his apparently innocent daughter. Although you'll work it all out soon enough the story is reasonably subtle at first and well developed. Christopher Lee could play these sort of stern pompous characters in his sleep and so he's perfect casting.

Nyree Dawn Porter, who plays the tutor in this segment, would return for more Amicus anthology capers in From Beyond the Grave. Chloe Franks, who plays young Jane in Sweets To The Sweet, was a busy child actor of this era and would appear in two more Amicus films - most famously as Joan Collins' daughter in Tales from the Crypt. Chloe Franks stopped acting in 1983 and later worked in helping people with disabilities get better education and employment. Franks is not the greatest child actor you'll ever see, she's not Bella Ramsey or Millie Bobby Brown, but she works quite well in Sweets to the Sweet and draws our sympathy early on. With Nyree Dawn Porter, Chloe Franks, Cushing and Lee back and an appearance by Geoffry Blaydon (who would memorably feature in the Amicus compendium Asylum) the studio is almost putting an unofficial repertory company of sorts in place for future productions.

Sweets to the Sweet is a decent little horror yarn with a suitably twisted ending. Nothing happens here that you didn't expect from the clues but it's fun anyway. This segment has quite an anachronistic and constrictive aura too which sets it apart from some (if not all) of the segments in the seventies anthology films that Amicus did. You could easily imagine

Sweets to the Sweet slotting into the 1965 film Dr Terror's House of Horrors and not being out of place at all.

The final story is called The Cloak and stars Jon Pertwee as a flamboyant horror film star named Paul Henderson who moves into the house as he prepares for his latest role. Although reduced to starring in low-budget clunkers like Curse of the Bloodsucker (his latest film), Henderson is still in possession of a massive ego and enjoys a (then) topical in-joke about Amicus rival Hammer. "That's what's wrong with the present day horror films," says Henderson. "There's no realism. Not like the old ones, the great ones. Frankenstein. Phantom of the Opera. Dracula - the one with Bela Lugosi of course, not this new fellow." The new fellow of course is Christopher Lee - also of course in The House That Dripped Blood.

Despite being an old ham, Henderson is a bit of a precious luvvie and to prepare fully for his new vampire role he visits a mysterious shop owned by the very odd Theo von Hartmann (Geoffrey Bayldon) to purchase a cloak befitting a man of his status and fame after rejecting the tattered one on offer from the film studio. "I'm Paul Henderson," he says modestly in the shop. "The great film actor." Henderson tries on a swanky theatrical cloak in the costume shop but this no ordinary cloak as he soon realises when his reflection immediately vanishes in the mirror...

Although fun, The Cloak is played mostly for laughs and this negates a little of the atmosphere despite a few nice twists and chills near the end. Jon Pertwee said that Milton Subotsky was furious when he saw the rushes of this segment because it was made as an undiluted comedy. Milton reminded them that The House That Dripped Blood was supposed to be a horror film - not a comedy. Some edits were subsequently made to The Cloak to make it less comedic. You have to wonder what the original version was like because the one that ended up in the film is fairly light and comedic. This segment is packed with little jokes about the film industry and low-budget horror films and it's certainly enjoyable to see Pertwee camping it up as Henderson and attempting to get a quick bite of Ingrid Pitt's buxom Carla.

Pertwee is a bit broad here but seems to be enjoying himself and while The Cloak isn't particularly scary it is of course good fun to see him and Ingrid Pitt together and Henderson's pompous on-set antics in the horror film (within a horror film) provide some nice jokes about the rather homemade but thriving British horror industry of the day. I would argue though that the 1976 Nigel Kneale anthology show Beasts did this sort of thing in a more interesting way with an episode called The Dummy *. The Cloak might not be the scariest segment Amicus ever committed to film but it does generate a lot of goodwill from the viewing with its knowing script and the presence of the likeable and charismatic Pertwee.

The House That Dripped Blood is good fun with a great cast and some decent stories. It isn't quite the best example of an Amicus anthology, perhaps lacking the creepy atmosphere of Tales From the Crypt and the sheer campy joy of Vault of Horror, with the framing device a slight disappointment too. That aside though, none of the stories is a complete clunker and the final twist/sequence at the end with Inspector Holloway's investigation (which wraps things up) is actually the most tense and scary bit of the film. The House That Dripped Blood is very enjoyable on the whole.

The House That Dripped Blood is actually the longest of the Amicus anthology films at 102 minutes but it doesn't feel like a long film and breezes past - supplying most of the fun and enjoyment you expect of one of these compendium capers. I find it difficult to rank the Amicus anthology films to be honest because, Torture Garden aside (which I think is a little bit weaker than the others - or at least not as much fun), I love all of them. The House That Dripped Blood is probably not my absolute favourite but it sits happily with Dr Terror's House of Horrors and the Amicus anthologies yet to come in this book as unbeatable late night retro horror entertainment.

* The Dummy was directed by Don Leaver. This is one of the best episodes of Beasts - Nigel Kneale's strange and unique anthology series. The story takes place on the set of a low budget horror film. An actor named Clyde Boyd (Bernard Horsfall) plays a dinosaur type monster known as 'Dummy'

but Clyde is in the midst of a nervous breakdown - not helped by the fact that one of the actors in the film has stolen his wife. Clyde is also drinking heavily and becoming increasingly temperamental but they have to keep him on the set in his monster suit to finish the film on time. He can't be replaced because the suit was fitted to his specifications and they can't afford another one. However, Clyde becomes increasingly distraught and frazzled, to the point where he can't seem to distinguish between himself and the monster anymore.

The Dummy is widely seen as Kneale having a not so sly pop at the sort of horror personified by Hammer (who Kneale didn't have much time for but then he didn't seem to have much time for anyone). The monster suit seems to be deliberately hokey but in a strange way it makes the story more effective when Cylde goes bonkers. When he goes on the rampage there is a rather cruel aura to the story knowing that someone could get hurt or worse by such a silly looking creature. This episode becomes increasingly dark as it progresses and it's very compelling. An actor in a monster suit going berserk on the set of a low budget horror film. It's a great premise. The Dummy is a very strange, dark and gripping episode and one of the strongest entries in this short lived but never forgotten series.

I, MONSTER (1971)

I, Monster was directed by Stephen Weeks and written by Milton Subotsky. It is based on The Strange Case of Dr Jekyll and Mr Hyde by Robert Louis Stevenson. The names Jekyll and Hyde are changed in the film. Christopher Lee plays Dr Charles Marlowe, a psychologist who becomes the wicked Edward Blake when he takes his new experimental serum. I suppose 'Dr Marlowe and Mr Blake' obviously wasn't a catchy enough title! The names Dr Jekyll and Mr Hyde were actually used though in the Italian dub of this film. Peter Cushing lends support as Marlowe's lawyer and friend Frederick Utterson. It is Utterson who suspects that all is not well with Dr Marlowe.

Stephen Weeks was only in his early twenties when he directed this film. He would go onto direct the 1974 British horror film Ghost Story and Sword of the Valiant - a 1983 Cannon film that had Sean Connery and Peter Cushing in the cast. After he finished Sword of the Valiant, Weeks started directing a film in India called The Bengal Lancers. The cast included Christopher Lee, Michael York, and Trevor Howard. The Bengal Lancers turned out to be an insurance scam by criminals and poor Stephen Weeks was the victim. Shortly into filming, the footage from the film was deemed out of focus and unusable by Technicolor - despite the fact that it was shot by a cameraman who had won an Oscar! It turned that someone had been bribed to send false reports on The Bengal Lancers footage. Anyway, to cut a long story short, there was a long legal battle and Stephen Weeks abandoned film directing to fight this battle. He had a dreadful time by all accounts thanks to this heartless Bengal Lancers scam.

I, Monster was a rather troubled production and shot in 3-D on the insistence of Milton Subotsky. The 3-D effect work was rendered useless though because the sets had been built the wrong way round. The 3-D was apparently one of the reasons why Peter Duffell turned down a chance to direct the picture. "In the case of I, Monster particularly, I turned that down for artistic reasons," said Duffell. "The film was made because Milton Subotsky had discovered what he thought was a cheap way of making a three-dimensional film.

"It involved the people coming into the cinema wearing a pair of those coloured glasses they did for 3D but with one lens missing. Well, people aren't going to sit in a cinema wearing those! Also, you had to have a constantly moving camera. And perhaps you got a kind of 3D effect. But I was against it because I don't believe a constantly moving camera is the right thing to do for a horror film. I mean, look at a James Whale movie. Very often it's a static camera. And so I was very unhappy about that, and I turned it down for that reason anyway. Milton subsequently did offer me one or two other pictures, but I held my position and said no, I didn't want to do them."

Stephen Weeks said that they ran out of money during the I,

Monster shoot (Weeks sarcastically suggested the budget was blown by painting the Amicus canteen - I personally like to think that Amicus had their own special horror themed canteen!) and Milton Subotsky simply told him to assemble what footage they did have and cut it into a film. With all this in mind, you might expect I, Monster to be terrible but it's actually a decent enough stab at adapting this famous story. One can certainly detect some padding in the film though with perhaps a few too many scenes of Cushing and others sitting around a gentlemen's club explaining the plot.

The Subotsky monologues about Freud and the superego (which the director apparently tried to chop away as much as he could) also feel a trifle clunky at times but - generally - the film is decent fun and along with And Now the Screaming Starts! is Amicus as its most Hammeresque. This is one of the few Amicus films where if you didn't know any better you might think it was made by Hammer. You can tell they didn't assemble much footage for this film because even the extended cut is only 81 minutes long! One slight problem with the film is a strange fuzzy glow effect, perhaps as a consequence of the rather bungled attempt to make a 3-D film.

Although the props and interiors are enjoyable and quite well done from a period point of view, this is not the most pristine or handsome looking horror film you've ever seen and lacks a certain polish. They update the 'potion' of the story and have Marlowe injecting himself. There are some modern flourishes in the screenplay and Marlowe is depicted as a man ahead of his time. He seems to be frustrated by priggish Victorian attitudes. "Suppose that, just for a while, we could let loose the reins, fulfil our desires without restriction, without control."

There's a wonderfully melodramatic score by Carl Davis and the costumes and designs are all very competent for a modestly budgeted film. The lack of money does show at times with the reliance on interiors but they do a decent job considering the constraints they were working under. The fact that the film wasn't finished doesn't really show too jarringly in the finished product. Luckily, it appears that they had some sort of ending in the can. When you read about the production issues this film (Peter Cushing was apparently on record as saying this was one of his least favourite films to work on) suffered from you'd expect it to be terrible but it isn't bad at all really and if you like Peter Cushing and Christopher Lee - and who doesn't? - then they alone make it worthy of your time.

Christopher Lee is front and centre here and gives, as one would expect, a very commanding performance as the curious and refined Marlowe. When he adopts scruffy hair and oversized teeth for the wicked Mr Blake, he seems to be genuinely enjoying himself. It's rare to see a film where Christopher Lee smiles so much! They don't really have elaborate transformation scenes in the film (lack of money?) and although Lee looks a little comical at times as the wicked Dr Blake, the make-up is largely effective.

Look out for Susan Jameson (aka Esther in New Tricks) being turned from a prim repressed woman into a raving nymphomaniac by Marlowe's potion. Richard Hurndall, who plays Lanyon in this film, is best remembered for replacing William Hartnell in the role of the First Doctor for Doctor Who's 20th anniversary special The Five Doctors. Peter Cushing plays a by now familiar part for him in I, Monster as the worried friend who must turn sleuth to work out what is going on. He's very much the supporting player here though. I suspect they didn't hire Cushing for very long on this film and just got him to come in for a few days and shoot a batch of scenes.

If you were expecting this to be a Lee/Cushing film where they both have an equal spotlight and share the story you might be slightly disappointed. Marlowe's science lab is fun in the film and it's enjoyable when he goes crackers and ends up having fights with knife wielding tearaways in alleys and that sort of stuff. The strong performance of Lee stops the film from descending into camp or ever becoming too silly to the point where you feel like you are watching a Two Ronnies sketch. You wouldn't call I, Monster a lost classic but it's perfectly watchable with a good cast and a fairly good sense of period and atmosphere. One might even say this was one of the more underrated of the many Amicus horror films.

TALES FROM THE CRYPT (1972)

Tales from the Crypt is the best known of the Amicus anthology films and was based on the infamous and influential (everyone from Stephen King to George Romero grew up loving them) 1950s EC horror and suspense comics published by William Gaines. The enjoyably lurid and colourful comics (which were rather gruesome and risque - although tongue-in-cheek and with their own twisted sense of karma and morality) offercd all manner of deaths, monsters, zombies, murders, ghosts, and general macabre mayhem stirred by greed, lust and envy until parents began to notice what their children were reading and the comics were banned - even becoming the subject of Congressional subcommittee hearings. The comics later spawned an enjoyable HBO anthology series called Tales from the Crypt in the 1990s but it was Milton Subotsky and Max Rosenberg who brought them to the screen first. Subotsky wrote the screenplay himself and based the stories on The Vault of Horror #35, Tales from the Crypt #23, The Haunt of Fear #12, Tales from the Crypt #46, and The Haunt of Fear #22 (which was a variation on W. W. Jacobs' famous short story The Monkey's Paw).

The film was allocated a budget of £170,000 and had a longer than usual shooting duration. Peter Duffell passed on the offer to direct Tales from the Crypt and so opened the door for Freddie Francis (who obviously must have patched up any differences he had with Milton Subotsky) to return to Amicus. Once again an interesting cast was assembled by the studio. Peter Cushing returned and even changed his part after reading the screenplay. Cushing was slated to play the role taken by Richard Greene in the film but asked if he could instead play Arthur Grimsdyke in the Poetic Justice segment. So the character of Grimsdyke (originally a minor non-speaking part) was fleshed out for Cushing and given dialogue and more story and scenes.

The talented (if troubled) Ian Hendy, a mid-career Joan

Collins, Ralph Richardson (who shot his contribution as the Crypt Keeper in one day), stage veteran Nigel Patrick, former star Richard Greene, and Amicus favourites Patrick Magee and Geoffrey Bayldon were all added to the colourful cast. According to Milton Subotsky, Christopher Lee was not asked to do Tales from the Crypt because he was more expensive to hire than Peter Cushing and his fee would have eaten into a chunk of the film's budget. The part of the coal hearted (or should that be NO hearted!) neighbour James Elliot in the Poetic Justice segment was supposed to be played by Ralph Bates but he was unavailable and replaced by Robin Phillips. Bates appeared in a fair few horror films elsewhere - most notably for Hammer.

Highgate Cemetery was used for the atmospheric cemetery scenes at the start of the film. Highgate Cemetery would also later be used in From Beyond the Grave. The home of Richard Greene in the segment Wish You Were Here was later used as the house of Gregory Peck in the horror film The Omen. The underground catacombs you see in the framing sequence for Tales from the Crypt were built for the archaeology themed EMI horror film Tower of Evil (aka Horror on Snape Island) which starred, among others, Jill Haworth, Anthony Valentine, Jack Watson, and Sir Robin of Askwith. Tower of Evil was made at Shepperton Studios around the same time as Tales from the Crypt and the two films shared one another's sets. Tower of Evil is a bit forgotten these days but you could argue that it is a very early example of a slasher film.

Tales from the Crypt was the first Amicus film I can ever remember watching as a child and so this film has a special place in my heart. To this day, the film is something of a Christmas Eve tradition for me. There is nothing quite like an Amicus anthology film at Christmas late at night in the dead of winter. The film opens with shots around an old graveyard and Bach's Toccata and Fugue in D minor. It's an Amicus Production, it's the seventies, and you know you are in for some kitsch retro fun. As usual, we get short horror tales all linked together by a framing device, in this case it's five strangers visiting some labyrinthine underground catacombs - which is a strange tourist attraction if you ask me. Sounds like a nightmare if you are claustrophobic! Geoffrey Bayldon plays the guide. They become a bit lost and end up in a strange 'skull' room where the door shuts behind them.

The monkish Crypt Keeper appears, played by none other than Ralph Richardson, and, in an old thesp in a seventies horror film sort of way, begins to talk about their future and respective fates. The terrible things they've done or are thinking of doing. If you are an Amicus anthology fan you know the drill by now. You know EXACTLY where this is heading and that's all part of the fun. I love the way Ralph Richardson plays the Crypt Keeper here with a bored indifference (which was probably genuine!) as if he just wants to get this finished as soon as he can and go down the pub or something. It actually suits the character perfectly! You get the impression that the Crypt Keeper has had quite a few of these dodgy characters due for a comeuppance in his skull room before so you can understand if he's getting a bit weary of doing this.

The underground caves are the perfect way to begin this film. It is wonderfully atmospheric as we go through the graveyard and then down into the catacombs. Tales from the Crypt is the first of the Amicus anthology films which goes for that camp, very 1970s aura at times and this is great fun. By the way, if you watch the Joan Collins character very closely in the opening wraparound there is a very big clue as to the fate of these characters. A certain item she is wearing - which we see her take in the opening segment. The opening segment in question is called '...And All Through The House' * and features good old Joan Collins as a woman named Joanne Clayton.

Joan was having a career crisis around this time but the home grown horror industry was on hand and would soon lead to her being involved in a love triangle with a tree and Michael Jayston in Tales That Witness Madness. It is Christmas Eve and carol singers sing sweetly from a very seventies radio as the camera pans around an equally seventies piece of interior decor. Joanne's husband Richard (Martin Boddey) settles down with a newspaper to enjoy this lovely moment of seasonal calm and anticipation... before blood splatters over his paper and we cut to Joanne looking very pleased with herself and holding a fireplace poker. Yes, she's done away with him for the insurance but can she cover her tracks and make it look like an accident? And what was that local newsflash on the radio? A homicidal maniac has just escaped? Dressed as Father Christmas? You'd better make sure all of those windows and doors are locked...

Joan Collins later said she never enjoyed making horror films very much and when the trashy softcore films The Bitch and The Stud made money and she got a part in the glossy American soap opera Dynasty she was glad to bid the horror industry farewell. I suspect the final straw for Joan was the 1976 Bert I Gordon film Empire of the Ants - where she's up to her neck in swamp water and in one of the worst films ever made. Here's the thing though. Joan Collins, with her larger than life persona, archness, and sex appeal was absolutely brilliant in horror films. Joan spends much of this first Tales from the Crypt segment alone with no dialogue but is always watchable. She has some wonderful panto facial expressions at various points and must have one of the finest smirks of all time.

Chloe Franks plays the young daughter Carol in the segment. Carol keeps coming downstairs to see if Santa has been yet - which as you might imagine is a pain for Joanne because she's trying to hide her husband's body and wash up the blood. As if that wasn't enough she's also got an escaped lunatic dressed as Father Christmas lurking around the house and looking for a way in. Joanne can't phone the police for help because she's just murdered her husband! Suffice to say, Joanne's murder plan definitely needed a bit more thought before she walloped her poor husband in the canister with that poker. The Christmas atmosphere adds to the creepiness of the segment (even the carols on the radio sound strangely eerie) and they make good use of snow, rattly windows and sound effects in his one. There is one really good moment that will make you jump too.

The homicidal Father Christmas (played by Oliver MacGreevy) in this segment is absolutely terrifying if you ask me. He's often not much more than a grubby face (or white beard in this case) peeping in through the window. What is really odd by the way is how the 1984 slasher film Silent Night, Deadly Night kicked up a big rumpus by having the killer dressed as Father Christmas. Had these complaining people in 1984 not seen Tales from the Crypt? It isn't as if Silent Night, Deadly Night was the first film to do this. Other films, like Christmas Evil and the bizarre British slasher Don't Open till Christmas, had also conflated Santa with horror long before Silent Night, Deadly Night. Anyway, this first segment does a pretty good job of maintaining some suspense over its short running time and although it doesn't have a tremendously surprising ending it is a great opening story for the anthology.

The next segment, Reflection Of Death, features Ian Hendry as Carl Maitland and is an adequate enough second portion of compendium capers. We see Carl emotionally saying goodbye to his children as they snooze away in their bunk beds at the start of this segment. Carl, the bounder, is walking out on them and his wife to be with young bit on the side secretary Susan (played by Angela Grant - who appeared in four Carry On films). They drive away down the motorway at night but are involved in a crash that spins the car over several times. Carl wakes up and staggers away from the wreckage to find help. The problem is, every person he meets or tries to flag down just screams at the mere sight of him. What has happened to Carl to make him so frightening? Well, I think I might have a theory.

Reflection Of Death is less campy than some of the other segments in Tales from the Crypt and fairly gripping to boot. I quite like this segment because it is all about atmosphere rather than story so feels like something slightly different. It looks really good in places, especially in the aftermath of the car smash with flames and a blurry light. They shoot everything from Carl's perspective so the reactions of everyone to him are scarier and more intriguing, making it all a trifle creepier. There is a 'revelation' shot that will make you jump a little if you've never seen it before and overall it's quite a tight and interesting story.

Ian Hendry did some terrific work in horror films in this decade. He was memorable in both Theatre of Blood and

Captain Kronos - Vampire Hunter. You wouldn't say that Tales from the Crypt was up there with those other performances because he doesn't get to say an awful lot in Reflection of Death but the mere presence of Hendry nonetheless lends this segment some extra class and gravitas. The ending is a bit of a cop out though and, like some other characters in these films, you do wonder what exactly was so terrible about Carl's behaviour for him to end up in front of the Crypt Keeper. He didn't kill anyone, he just left his wife!

The next segment Poetic Justice features the great Peter Cushing, here giving a very endearing and sweet performance as a kind old widower called Arthur Grymsdyke who makes toys for the local children and looks after a huge menagerie of stray cats and dogs that help alleviate his loneliness. Arthur's ramshackle house though is situated in an increasingly upmarket neighbourhood and snobby posh git James Elliot (Robin Phillips) from across the road finds himself more and more irritated by having this eccentric and slightly disorganised old man living near him and ruining the view. Elliot begins a campaign to remove the old man and becomes more and more cold-hearted in his obsessive quest to drive Grymsdyke out of the neighbourhood.

Ah, James Elliot. Surely the most detestable villain in any of these anthology films. If anyone deserves some nasty horror anthology cosmic karma it is Mr Elliot. Arthur Grymsdyke is just about the nicest man in the world. He's kind to the local children and helps rescue animals. He's a gentle soul who doesn't have a bad bone in his body. What drives the irrational hatred of Elliot towards Grymsdyke is snobbery and class. Elliot lives with his father Edward (David Markham) in a big house across the road. He has a fancy book lined study and a roaring log fire. Elliot acts as if he's a character in Brideshead Revisited and having this elderly dustman living across the road is more than he can stand. James Elliot is George Osborne levels of dislikability. He's just the worst person in the world.

There is nothing the sociopathic Elliot won't stoop to in his quest to drive Grymsdyke away. He has the animals Grymsdyke owns taken and even lies to the local parents that the old man makes toys for the kids for less than innocent reasons. Rest assured though. This is an Amicus anthology film so Elliot is going to pay a heavy price for all of his evil meddling and scheming. Peter Cushing is wonderful as usual in Poetic Justice and always very watchable. His incredibly sympathetic performance is a major plus here. Cushing's character echoed his own grief for his late wife and he certainly pulls on the heartstrings. Grymsdyke's late wife has the same name as Cushing's late wife - Helen. **

There is a scene that is almost too sad to watch when Grymsdyke reads out horrible Valentines cards sent to him by Elliot. I find the bit where Grymsdyke is having his dinner alone with a photo of his wife on the table very moving. There's a nice visual contrast here as Grymsdyke has a humble pot of tea on the table with his dinner whereas Elliot is a pretentious berk who has decanters of sherry in his house. The grisly ending is very satisfying in Poetic Justice and great fun. This segment does come the closest I feel to evoking the spirit of EC Comics. You've got all the classic ingredients here. A truly horrible villain and a gruesome coda where just desserts are served. I'm not entirely sure that Carl Maitland deserved to end up in front of the Crypt Keeper but the same most assuredly cannot be said of James Elliot!

The next segment, Wish You Were Here, is a variation on 'The Monkey's Paw' and not bad. Richard Greene plays a businessman called Ralph Jason who is struggling to keep his finances above water. Barbara Murray, as his wife, finds a Chinese antique and wishes for a fortune to help them out. This has rather unfortunate consequences for her husband to say the least. Wish You Were Here is a decent enough, though weird segment, with quite a shocking conclusion. It has a good creepy atmosphere throughout although it is slightly inconsistent in tone, with a bit where some pallbearers are carrying a coffin into a house coming across like something out of an Eric Sykes skit.

This story in Wish You Were Here doesn't actually make an awful lot of sense when you think about it afterwards but to analyse films like this too much is probably to miss the point - and fun. One fun element to this one is seeing 'Death' following Greene on a motorcycle, quite literally, as they race through the countryside of Amicus Land! Richard Greene, a former matinee idol who played Robin Hood on television, is well cast as the suave businessman. The first time I watched this film I didn't understand why Ralph Jason ended up in front of the Crypt Keeper. It transpires though that Jason is a very dodgy businessman who has dabbled in arms sales and gun-running.

What helps this segment a lot is the cast. Roy Dotrice is great as the voice of reason lawyer who warns Mrs Jason to choose her three wishes very carefully - wise words which will almost certainly not be heeded because this is a horror film and horrible things are bound to happen. Barbara Murray is suitably frantic near the end as Mrs Jason and the cast manage to lift up what is a fairly familiar sort of horror story. Wish You Were Here is probably the least memorable of the segments in Tales from the Crypt but it certainly isn't bad and has a memorably twisted ending.

The best is - in my opinion - saved for last in Tales from the Crypt with Blind Alleys. "In the kingdom of the blind the one-eyed man is King," says Major William Rogers, wonderfully played by Nigel Patrick. Rogers has taken over as the new boss of Elmridge Home For the Blind, an anachronistic, ramshackle institution that is apparently always surrounded by snow and a howling wind. Rogers immediately begins a new cost cutting operation which involves a reduction on the heating and food for the residents. But the Major is making no such concessions in his own office - which he is even buying new paintings for!

The scene where Major Rogers is seen tucking into a huge lunch beside a roaring fire in his office after the frozen blind folk have been fobbed off with watery soup in the canteen is probably one of the funniest in cinema history. "Why don't you all go to bed?" says the incredibly tactful and sensitive Major when they complain about the lack of heating. "You can't see anything anyway." One man who definitely isn't going to stand for this is George Carter (Patrick Magee). When one of the blind old folks dies due to the cold, Carter and the other residents of Elmridge are soon plotting what becomes a somewhat implausible but enjoyable revenge.

Blind Alleys works as a very black comedy and veers more into horror near the end. The segment is deliberately and enjoyably anachronistic (the home for the blind is like something from 1872) and is powered by Nigel Patrick as the oblivious and uncaring Rogers and Magee as the formidable and increasingly outraged Carter. I love the bit where the blind folk need food to distract Shane, the alsation dog of Rogers, so they each contribute a bit of their breakfast and pass it along! The sequence where the residents construct an elaborate and deadly trap for Rogers is not very realistic but it's all part of the fun. Major Rogers is a classic Amicus anthology panto villain.

We then return to the catacombs where the fate of all these characters is revealed - and that fate will surely come as no surprise to Amicus fans. The special effects in this last bit are a trifle on the dodgy side but it doesn't really matter. I quite like the way the Crypt Keeper breaks the fourth wall at the end and wonders if we might be his next guests. There's only one sure way to avoid that fate. Be a nice person! It is only wicked horrible people who end up in the catacombs.

Tales From The Crypt is campy, very British fun with one or two twists and turns and a couple of good shocks. Freddie Francis always manages to make to film look interesting with bright garish colours in some scenes and an eerie fog in others and the cast is good fun, taking in everyone from Joan Collins to Patrick Magee. There have been many horror anthology films made since 1972 but few are as enjoyable as Tales from the Crypt.

* '...And All Through The House' was later remade for HBO's enjoyable 1990s anthology show Tales from the Crypt. If you watch the first season of HBO's Tales from the Crypt, well, here is that story again, only this time with an American setting and Robert Zemeckis behind the camera rather than Freddie Francis. It's Christmas Eve and housewife Elizabeth (Mary Ellen Trainor) puts her young daughter (played by Lindsey Whitney Barry) to bed and then whacks her unsuspecting husband Joseph (Marshall Bell) over the head with the fireplace poker. The murderous Elizabeth is after the

life insurance but she has missed a local news bulletin about a dangerous escapee (played by Larry Drake) from the asylum who is at large and dressed as Father Christmas. When Elizabeth is attacked by the insane Santa outside she manages to get back inside and lock the door. Only then does she realise that she left the body of her murdered husband out in the snow. It means she can't call the police and must now deal with this deranged Father Christmas alone. Will she survive?

HBO's And All Through the House does unavoidably lose the element of surprise if you've seen the Amicus film and the Joan Collins version but this is still well worth watching and is regarded by many to be one of the best Tales from the Crypt episodes. The main difference with this one is that they open it up more with some of the action taking place in the yard outside. The Amicus adaptation was strictly Joan Collins in her house and had more claustrophobia. While it looks like a slam dunk to cast Larry Drake as a murderous Father Christmas (and it is a slam dunk because Drake is great here) I do feel the Santa in the Amicus film was scarier because we hardly saw him save for a grubby bearded face at the window. Anyway, both versions are perfectly fine and this one is certainly fun too - especially if you are completely new to And All Through the House in any form.

Another EC Comics story from this film that was remade for HBO's Tales from the Crypt is Blind Alleys. In the television show the story is called Revenge is the Nuts and was directed by Jonas McCord and written by Shel Willens. Revenge is the Nuts doesn't work quite as well as Blind Alleys if you ask me. Veteran baddie Anthony Zerbe takes the Nigel Patrick role here, playing a scumbag named Arnie Grunwald who runs a shelter for the blind but is unfailingly cruel to them. Cutting rations, turning off the heat and light etc. When new resident Shelia (Teri Polo) is asked to sleep with Grunwald in exchange for better conditions for those in the home, this turns out to be the last straw and revenge is in the air.

The first season HBO Tales from the Crypt update of And All Through the House was great but Revenge is the Nuts (a terrible title) is much harder work. The home for the blind here has precious little atmosphere or authenticity and it only seems to have about five residents. In the Amicus film at least they had extras for scenes in the canteen. Zerbe is fine although this is the type of role he could probably have done in his sleep. Patrick Magee is sorely missed but you do get Isaac Hayes and Bibi Besch (Carol Marcus in Star Trek II: The Wrath of Khan). The last act is more or less the same as the Amicus segment but - like the episode as a whole - just not as much fun.

By the way, the last season of HBO's Tales from the Crypt had another variation on The Monkey's Paw which was directed by Freddie Francis and called Last Respects. It was written by Scott Nimerfro. Francis of course directed 1972's Tales from the Crypt so a nice touch to get him to direct an episode when production of this HBO series moved to Blighty for its last year. Sadly though, Last Respects is hardly the most memorable Tales from the Crypt. It's another version of the Monkey's Paw short story by WW Jacobs and concerns three sisters - LaVonne (Emma Samms), Delores (Kerry Fox), and Marlice (Julie Cox) - who run an old curiosity shop and stumble across one (a Monkey's Paw that is).

Aware of the legend surrounding said object, they start wishing and realise that magical properties truly are afoot. However, to state the bleeding obvious in this case, you should be very careful what you wish for because it might just come true. The story is at least Tales from the Crypt in spirit and the predictable finale is fun but Last Respects always feels like much harder work than it should be with some hysterical mugging by the cast. One senses that the British actors have been told that Tales from the Crypt is a tongue-in-cheek show and then gone a bit overboard with this instruction. Tales from the Crypt was always a very tongue-in-cheek show but that doesn't excuse bad acting. Just calm down everyone.

** In 1986, Peter Cushing published a very personal autobiography that included much material about his late wife Helen. Helen died in 1971 and Cushing never really recovered, often saying in interviews that he was merely biding his time now until they were united again. The first part of the memoir includes Cushing talking about how devastated he was by the death of his wife. He says he actually ran up and down the stairs in the faint hope of inducing a heart attack and considered suicide. In the end though Cushing, a man of great faith, decided this would be wrong and said that he knows he will see her again one day. He admits he considered taking an indefinite break from acting but his friends told him it would be good for him to keep busy and it was what he did best. Cushing explains in the memoir how Helen played a crucial role in his career, encouraging him to keep going through some difficult periods.

WHAT BECAME OF JACK AND JILL? (1972)

What Became of Jack and Jill? was directed by Bill Bain and written by Roger Marshall. Roger Marshall was the writer on the brilliant private detective (or inquiry agent if you prefer) show Public Eye with Alfred Burke. Bill Bain was an Australian director who won acclaim for directing episodes of Upstairs, Downstairs and also Public Eye. What Became of Jack and Jill? is based on a novel called The Ruthless Ones by Laurence Moody.

What Became of Jack and Jill? was co-produced with Palomar and shelved for a year because no one knew what to do with it. It was made in 1971 but got a limited release in 1972. It was originally going to be called Romeo and Juliet '71 and the idea was that the film would be tailored for the grindhouse market in the United States and open up a new revenue stream for Amicus. Things didn't go according to plan though. What Became of Jack and Jill? is arguably the most obscure film in the Amicus catalogue.

What Became of Jack and Jill? is a very atypical Amicus film and feels like an attempt to make an exploitation picture with youth culture trappings. You wouldn't really call this a horror film. This is a rather difficult film to put into any specific category. If pushed, you might call it a psychological drama or a black comedy. The film revolves around Johnnie Tallent (Paul Nicholas). Johnnie is a workshy idle young man who lives with and looks after his grandmother Alice (Mona Washbourne). Alice has a heart condition and relies on Johnnie around the house.

Although his grandmother seems to regard him to be a nice young man who helps out and prevents her from feeling lonely, nothing could be further from the real truth. Johnnie is desperate for his grandmother to kick the bucket so he can inherit the house and her savings. Even more desperate for granny to shuffle off this mortal coil is Johnnie's cold hearted girlfriend Jill Standish (Vanessa Howard). Johnnie and Jill are already dreaming of the many ways they can spend granny's money so they hatch a plot to hasten her demise.

What Became of Jack and Jill? is only watchable for Vanessa Howard, an engagingly eccentric and natural actress who always oozes a slightly kooky sort of charisma. There were many young actresses who had parts in British horror films in the sixties and seventies but none were quite like Vanessa Howard. There is just something completely fascinating and arch about Vanessa Howard. If you gave her a decent part in a film then none of the other actors stood a chance. She would completely steal the show.

Sadly, the troubled nature around this time of both the release of What Became of Jack and Jill? and the obscure but brilliant Freddie Francis film Mumsy, Nanny, Sonny and Girly ended the career of the unique and always amazing Vanessa Howard. She was so disillusioned by the bungled release and obscurity of these two films (in which she does incredible work) that she gave up acting at the age of twenty-three. What Became of Jack and Jill? was her last film role. It's a great shame indeed that we never saw any more films with Vanessa Howard.

Apparently, Amicus had plans to make Vanessa Howard their new star - which was a nice idea. You can picture Vanessa Howard playing the Britt Ekland part in Asylum, the Stephanie Beacham part in And Now the Screaming Starts!, the Angela Pleasance part in From Beyond the Grave, and so on, but whether this would have made her a star is open to question. She certainly deserved to be a star though. I suspect that Vanessa Howard could have had a long Georgina Hale style career had she stuck at acting. Paul Nicholas, who for British audiences will always be best known as Vince Pinner in the 80s sitcom Just Good Friends, is not bad in the main role if a trifle wooden. He can't really keep pace with Vanessa Howard in the acting stakes but he's ok in the film.

The young Paul Nicholas was quite good in this sort of part. Outwardly charming but shallow and bitter below the surface. Mona Washbourne, as granny, has a rather thankless part in the film as her character is required to be incredibly gullible and react to some preposterous ruses cooked up by Johnnie. Johnnie tricks his grandmother into believing that there is some sort of revolutionary disaffected youth movement on the rise that is fed up with old folks having all the money and power. He pretends that a riot on television is part of this and graffitis 'Out with the Oldies' on the wall outside to further frighten his timid grandmother.

Johnnie even tells her that the youth movement is going to start coming around personally to apprehend the old folks and force them out of their homes - all of this nonsense designed to induce a heart attack (as granny has a dodgy ticker). This is by far the most ludicrous part of the film. It's hard to believe that anyone would be stupid enough to really fall for this! What Became of Jack and Jill? is not exactly the most eventful film you'll ever watch. The first half consists mostly of Johnnie and grandmother in their dingy house. Sometimes scenes are so dark you can barely make out the characters and that orange wallpaper is hideous!

This is one of those films where a decent print seems elusive. It never really had a proper DVD release (presumably because there was no particular demand). This is definitely the most kitchen sink film Amicus ever produced. The rather drab nature of the film does at least though make the dream sequences (where Johnnie and Jill daydream about being rich and cavort around with flash cars and diamonds) more arresting and there's quite a good scene near the start where the crooked couple are cavorting in a cemetery and snort one of granny's heart pills!

There's no getting away from the fact though that What Became of Jack and Jill? is a really odd film. It's hard to know who this is supposed to be aimed at. You have a few 'youth culture' disco scenes but then the very constrictive slow burn kitchen sink backdrop of that grotty house. Large chunks of the film consist of Mona Washbourne shuffling around the dark house as the scheming Paul Nicholas plots to get his grubby mitts on her money. Anyone expecting a horror film or a thriller is likely to be disappointed by What Became of Jack and Jill? but it is worth watching - if only for Vanessa Howard. She's just a very entertaining and offbeat presence in this film.

I especially like the scene where Jill quits her job at the travel agent and tells her boss to book a cruise right up his "back passage"! I also like the scene where Jill is chewing gum and comparing herself to a pin-up poster. Vanessa Howard makes this little throwaway moment weird, funny, and memorable. Vanessa Howard aside though, What Became of Jack and Jill? is a very strange little drama that never quite works or ever really seems to decide what it what wants to be. The ending is rather abrupt and the slow pacing of the film might be frustrating to some viewers.

What Became of Jack and Jill? is not a very good film and is a bit too weird for its own good at times but I would recommend watching it purely for the performance of Vanessa Howard as Jill. Both this film and Mumsy, Nanny, Sonny and Girly illustrate the vast potential that Howard had as an actor and potential star of the 1970s but sadly her career seemed to end before it had ever really taken off.

ASYLUM (1972)

The next of the Amicus anthology films saw the director's taken by Roy Ward Baker, an experienced hand responsible for genre films like Quatermass and the Pit, Dr Jekyll and Sister Hyde and Scars of Dracula. Douglas Gamley scored the film although he made much use of public domain pieces by Modest Mussorgsky. Peter Cushing returned but Christopher

Lee was absent this time. An interesting cast was assembled for Asylum, including a future star in Charlotte Rampling, big names somewhat on the way down in Richard Todd and Sylvia Sims, the always watchable Barry Morse and Patrick Magee, and a young Robert Powell and Britt Ekland.

Robert Powell was still in his twenties at the time and at the start of his career. Ralph Bates, Michael Jayston, and Tom Adams were among the actors that Powell beat to the central role of Dr Martin. In an interview on the set, Charlotte Rampling said she was enjoying making Asylum because there was none of the waiting around in boredom you get on other films. Amicus didn't faff around on their productions. They got these films in the can as efficiently as possible!

Britt Ekland was best known at the time for being the former wife of Peter Sellers. She had recently had a part in the cult gangster film Get Carter. Shortly after Asylum she would land her two most famous roles - Willow in The Wicker Man and Mary Goodnight in the Bond film The Man with the Golden Gun. Spike Milligan was supposed to play the orderly Max Reynolds in this film but he dropped out shortly before shooting began and was replaced by the ever reliable Geoffrey Bayldon. Herbert Lom (who became much more famous when the Pink Panther series was reactivated in the mid-1970s) apparently shot his contribution to Asylum in half a day! Asylum was made at Shepperton and locations in Berkshire and wrapped inside a month. It was another success and showed that was still life in the anthology horror franchise Amicus were carving out with singular determination.

The building used for the insane asylum in the film is New Lodge in Berkshire. New Lodge is a large historic mansion located adjacent to the western edge of Windsor Great Park and approximately four miles west of Windsor. The current mansion, built on the site of Henry VIII's hunting lodge, was constructed in 1857 in the neo gothic style. Robert Bloch supplied the stories for the film (where would horror/mystery anthology shows and films be without Robert Bloch?) though, as was his custom, he later aimed a few barbs at how they were handled.

Despite this though the reputation of Asylum as a film

seems to be very good these days. As far as anthology films go, Asylum is great stuff. Bloch said there was supposed to be a fifth segment in the film but this was cut from the script before shooting began - which is a shame. Amicus presumably did this to save a bit of money. Asylum was in cinemas about three and a half months after it started shooting! Asylum was called House of the Crazies in the United States releases. I much prefer Asylum as the title myself.

Asylum features four stories all linked by a framing device set at Dunsmoor Asylum for 'the incurably insane' and begins with young psychiatrist Dr Martin (Robert Powell) arriving at this isolated and bleak mist shrouded institution in his sleek sports car to the atmospheric strains of Night on Bald Mountain by Modest Mussorgsky. Martin is here for a job interview and is met by the weary, morose, wheelchair-bound head of the asylum Dr Rutherford, played by the always enjoyably eccentric Patrick Magee. The wraparound framing sequence in Asylum is excellent because it weaves into the film in a more natural and complex way than wraparounds in most anthology films.

Rutherford explains that he is in a wheelchair because of an attack by one of the patients ("Never turn your back on a patient!" he advises Dr Martin) and that "Dr Starr", a former member of staff, has developed a "dual personality" and is now insane and a patient himself. He sets Dr Martin a rather strange challenge. Martin must go and visit four patients in their rooms and if he guesses correctly which one is Dr Starr he can have the position he has come to be interviewed for. Our young job applicant takes up the challenge and makes his way to the patients with the asylum's orderly Max Reynolds (Geoffrey Bayldon). In familiar Amicus compendium tradition, we then see each story in a flashback as each patient tells Dr Martin how they ended up at Dunsmoor.

The first story is called Frozen Fear and features Richard Todd as Walter, a middle-aged man having an affair with young Bonnie (Barbara Parkins) - who tells the story to Dr Martin from her room in the asylum. Walter's main problem is his annoying nagging heiress wife Ruth (Sylvia Sims). He wants rid of her and his hands on some of her cash but she steadfastly refuses a divorce and mocks him for being stuck with her. A frustrated Walter cooks up a grisly plan that will make use of a big new fridge freezer he's bought and had put in the cellar and - this being an Amicus compendium film - it probably won't come as a huge surprise to know he didn't buy it to put the fish fingers and Arctic Roll in there. Meanwhile, Ruth has been studying voodoo, as you do. It's amazing some of the things they do now in evening classes!

Frozen Fear is an incredibly daft but enjoyable beginning to Asylum with heinous crimes being punished in EC Comics style. It's fun of course to see the stalwart screen war hero Richard Todd (who apparently regretted making Asylum if later interviews are anything to go by) in a somewhat camp horror segment wearing a quite extraordinary cravat and drinking copious amounts of brandy from comically huge glasses as he wanders around his seventies living room in a blue cardigan. The period trappings of these films are a big part of the fun and it really wouldn't be an Amicus anthology film without at least one decanter of brandy or some yellow wallpaper.

The climax of Frozen Fear is preposterous but it is all done with tongue firmly planted in cheek. Hokey voodoo elements were something of a tradition with Amicus and seemed to usually feature in at least one of the anthology segments in their films. Frozen Fear has a few good lines ("Rest in pieces!") and is good fun on the whole if you can keep a straight face during some of the more far out interludes. Though I doubt that Richard Todd and Sylvia Sims would have given Asylum pride of place in their memoirs they are both - professionals that they were - good in the film. Barbara Parkins is also well cast as the young woman who is the catalyst for the fridge related horrors which abound in this segment. Amicus were very shrewd in their casting in the way they would hire a big name and then shoot their scenes in a day or two. You could say they were ahead of their time because these dire straight to DVD (or VOD if you prefer) films today commonly use that tactic. Frozen Fear is as daft as a brush and hugely entertaining.

The next story is called The Weird Tailor * and is probably

the highlight of the film. Bruno (Barry Morse of Space 1999 fame) is a tailor with huge grey mutton-chop sideburns who looks like he's just stepped out of another century. Now a shambling nervous wreck reduced to air sewing invisible garments in his room at the asylum, he recounts his terrible tale to Dr Martin. What on earth could have happened to Bruno to reduce him to this? We cut to a dark, foggy, anachronistic London backstreet where Bruno works in his little tailor's shop. The problem is, the impoverished Bruno is skint and his nasty landlord is threatening him and his wife Anna (Ann Firbank) over the rent owed.

Bruno is desperate and very worried but things perk up when the mysterious Mr Smith (Peter Cushing) enters his shop and requests that a suit be made for him. This is no ordinary suit though. It's to be made out of a strange luminous material and Mr Smith has very precise instructions. It can only be worked on after midnight and an astrological deadline is imposed. Bruno, eager for the revenue, begins work according to the stipulations laid down. But who is Mr Smith and why all the strange rules?

The Weird Tailor is great fun and quickly develops into quite a compelling mystery. You do get drawn in as Bruno slavishly works on the suit and find yourself very eager to find out what the purpose of it is and what Mr Smith is up to. The strange, fluorescent material is a pleasant weird touch and Barry Morse, despite his comedy accent and rather anachronistic appearance, is good value as the nervous Bruno, a meek tailor who wonders what he is stumbling into but just needs the money to keep his business and home. Morse was quite an interesting actor and capable of playing different types of roles.

Peter Cushing is always enjoyable in anything and is suitably enigmatic and crisp as the mysterious Mr Smith. It's interesting when Cushing is given a morally dubious character to play and his performance is very good. The story is a fun one anyway but the performances of Cushing and Morse - as two quietly desperate men - make it even more enjoyable. The final twist in The Weird Tailor is excellent and provides Asylum with perhaps its most memorable moment. By the way, Ann Firbank, who plays Bruno's wife in this segment, is still acting in her nineties and recently appeared in Star Wars: The Rise of Skywalker. She was also in 1963's The Servant - which might just be my favourite film.

The next story, Lucy Comes To Stay, is, like all the tales on offer here, an adaption of one of Bloch's short stories. It's alright and generates a surreal atmosphere at times but it isn't my favourite in the film by a long way. The pacing is far too slow and the twist too obvious. Barbara (Charlotte Rampling) tells her story to Dr Martin in flashback and we cut to a plush country house where Barbara is staying with her posh bowler hat and umbrella brother George (James Villiers) and her Nurse Miss Higgins (Megs Jenkins) after being released from another institution. Barbara however has a 'friend' called Lucy (Britt Ekland) and Lucy tends to be a very bad influence on Barbara (and that's putting it mildly). Is the mischievous Lucy real or a figment of Barbara's imagination?

The presence of a young Charlotte Rampling is a help here in what is not the most exciting anthology segment Amicus ever served up. Rampling must be one of the coolest actors that Amicus ever persuaded to be in one of their films because her star was on the rise and she would go on to become a great actor. Imagine if Amicus had persuaded Vanessa Howard to play the Lucy part in this film. Charlotte Rampling and Vanessa Howard together! That would have been great. Anyway, they try to keep you guessing in this story at first by making everything somewhat vague. You can probably spot the ending a mile off but it develops a bit of tension and does have a mildly creepy moment at its conclusion.

Britt Ekland, let's be honest, probably not the world's greatest ever actor, is a potential liability here but her wholesome Scandinavian good looks and slightly wooden acting style help to give off an air of weirdness that, whether intentional or not, works to a degree. James Villiers, who played James Bond's temporary boss Tanner in For Your Eyes Only, and Meg Jenkins (who will always be Mrs Baithwaite in Worzel Gummidge to me) are both fine in their supporting roles. Lucy Comes To Stay might have been better placed as the second segment to be honest. It does come off as a trifle dull immediately after The Weird Tailor but may have worked better coming directly after Frozen Fear. Lucy Comes To Stay just seems to lack something and isn't as memorable as the other stories in Asylum.

The last story is called Mannikins of Horror and becomes part of the end of the film in the asylum rather than a flashback. The patient this time is none other than Herbert Lom (in a very camp artist's gown outfit) as "Dr Byron". The pompous Byron, who still acts as if he is a respected doctor rather than an asylum inmate ("A pleasure to meet a colleague!" he booms to Dr Martin), is making good use of his spare time in the asylum though. In fact, he's making miniature robot puppets that he claims are replicas of humans! The final step will be to "will them into existence". To be fair to him, it's something we've all tried to do on that rainy Sunday afternoon when you find yourself at a loose end.

This rather novel final segment is incredibly silly, even for Amicus, but again good fun, not least for the presence of Herbert Lom. Anyone with fond memories of the Pink Panther films will laugh as soon as he appears. Dr Martin decides to call it a day (and someone showing you their collection of robot puppets is probably likely to have that effect) and wearily heads back to see Dr Rutherford. However, there are still plenty of twists, turns and surprises in store as the big secret of the film begins to unravel. We will finally find out the identity of Dr Starr...

One of the strengths of Asylum is that the framing device is interesting and doesn't come across as too contrived. Dr Martin is actually interviewing these patients to work out who Dr Starr is so it makes perfect sense for him to hear their stories. Although Asylum is quite campy and daft, the ending of the film is creepy (and the asylum generally is a creepy setting) and very enjoyable, wrapping things up nicely as we finally learn who Dr Starr is. The theme of this film seems to be inanimate objects and the addition of usual staples like voodoo and anachronistic period touches all help to maintain the spooky aura. The use of public domain pieces by Modest Mussorgsky adds greatly to the atmosphere too and there is stirring music by Douglas Gamley.

Robert Powell is well cast as the idealistic Dr Martin in the framing sections and his exchanges with Patrick Magee are always enjoyable as Martin gradually begins to realise Rutherford might be as nutty as his patients. In addition to Powell and Rutherford, Peter Cushing, Barry Morse and Geoffrey Bayldon are all excellent value. Although none of the Amicus anthologies were ever likely to win an Oscar, the direction is solid enough and there are some good little touches - like the macabre medical lithographs that grace the walls as Dr Martin makes his way upstairs to the patients. Asylum is a lot of fun for Amicus fans everywhere.

* The Weird Tailor was previously adapted for the screen in 1961 as part of the Boris Karloff fronted anthology show Thriller. This television version was directed by Herschel Daugherty and written by Robert Bloch (obviously adapting his own story). Mr Smith (George Macready) is performing a darkly magical black mass when his drunken son arrives home unexpectedly and is killed in what we can only call a black mass related incident! Smith is distraught but after consulting psychic Madam Roberti (Iphigenie Castiglioni) he manages to obtain a rare book which he believes will allow him to bring his son back from the dead. With a very strange glowing material, Smith visits the penniless tailor Erich Borg (Henry Jones) and says he will pay him $500 if he fashions a suit from the material and only work at certain hours in accordance with 'astrological' guidelines.

Erich, who owes landlord Mr Schwenk (Stanley Adams) money, is delighted to have an apparently wealthy customer and sets to work on this most unusual task. His wife Anna (Sondra Blake) is not so sure though. She thinks there is something about this that doesn't feel right. Both the Amicus and Thriller versions of this story are great fun and worth watching but if pressed you'd have to say that the Thriller version is scarier - especially at the end. This version is longer than the one in Asylum as Bloch expanded it with scenes and details absent from the later Amicus adaptation. So you get the scenes with the clairvoyant and also Smith purchasing the 'De Vermis Mysteriis' book.

What you also get much more of in this version is the tailor's wife. Erich is absolutely beastly to her and practically the first time we see her he slaps her for no apparent reason. This is a big change from the Amicus adaptation in which Barry Morse's tailor was more gentle and sympathetic. In this version the tailor is a despicable and cruel little man. The one advantage the Amicus version has is the great Peter Cushing as Smith. George Macready is terrific but Cushing is hard to beat and I thought the vague nature of Smith in the Amicus version was probably more effective (in that we had no idea why he wanted the suit made or what he was up to until the end). Anyway, the tailor's wife (superbly played by Sondra Blake) is fleshed out more in the Thriller version and we get scenes of her talking to the shop dummy Hans. She's so lonely and starved of affection he's almost like her secret lover.

Hans is credited as Diki Lerner and you can clearly see him moving at times when Sondra Blake is venturing forth these heartfelt monologues about her sad life to him. They should have just used a real dummy for these scenes I think. These minor distractions do not in any form detract though from what is a fantastic 50 minutes of anthology horror fun. There are fine performances all round and the final scene is creepier than the one in the Amicus version simply because of the strange movement it involves. I like the little details in this story too that you notice on close inspection. The landlord Mr Schwenk seems relentless and ruthless seeking his money but note how when he encounters Erich in a bar drowning his sorrows that Schwenk is shown to be capable of compassion. The Weird Tailor is certainly one of the most enjoyable of the horror themed Thriller episodes and well worth watching.

VAULT OF HORROR (1973)

Tales from the Crypt was so successful that a sequel anthology - Vault of Horror - featuring more EC stories was rushed into production. The Crypt Keeper was dispensed with this time and Roy Ward Baker returned to Amicus to direct the film.

The stories chosen were taken from Tales from the Crypt #35, Shock SuspenStories #1, Tales from the Crypt #33, Tales from the Crypt #28, and Tales from the Crypt #26. Peter Cushing was absent from an Amicus anthology for the first time in Vault of Horror as he was busy filming And Now the Screaming Starts! - also an Amicus film.

Vault of Horror is also known as The Vault of Horror. I prefer Vault of Horror rather than the slightly longer title (which would explain why I'm using it in this book). The film was called Further Tales from the Crypt and Tales from the Crypt II in some American re-releases. I've occasionally noticed that Vault of Horror seems to be regarded as one of the weakest of the Amicus anthology films in retrospectives. This not a perception though that I've ever shared myself. Vault of Horror is an absolute blast if you love retro British horror anthology films. This film is pure fun if you ask me. At 83 minutes it isn't very long but this does mean that the pacing is snappy and it breezes past without ever threatening to lose your interest.

The respected stage and screen actor Daniel Massey was signed for Vault of Horror alongside his sister Anna while Tom Baker and German-Austrian actor Curt Jürgens (both yet to play their most famous roles as Doctor Who and the villain Stromberg in the James Bond adventure The Spy Who Loved Me respectively) were also added to the cast. The popular and well known comic character actor Terry-Thomas also signed to appear in Vault of Horror although, sadly, Thomas had just been diagnosed with Parkinson's disease and his career was now on a downward slope.

Robin Nedwell and Geoffrey Davies, who appear in the segment titled Bargain in Death, were well known to British audiences from the comedy show Doctor in the House. Michael Craig, who also appears in the Bargain in Death segment, was already a veteran of many British films. Michael Craig was one of those actors who never became a big star - despite constantly working all the time. I always remember Michael Craig as the sadistic prison commandant (who is pointedly named Thatcher!) in the violent 1982 Ozploitation film Turkey Shoot.

The modern office block which you see at the start of Vault of Horror, and in which the wraparound takes place (though the interior was obviously depicted in a studio), is Millbank Tower. Millbank Tower sits beside the River Thames, half a mile upstream from the Palace of Westminster. It was built in 1963 so would have still been a fairly new building when Vault of Horror was made. It was from offices in Millbank Tower that Tony Blair's Labour Party orchestrated the general election campaign in 1997 which saw them win a landslide majority.

Vault of Horror was bloodier than the other Amicus compendiums and cuts were made in order to gain a lower certificate (and so gain a wider audience). Unfortunately the cut version of Vault of Horror became the 'standard' version for many years and it was only in 2008 that the uncut original version of was shown on British television for the first time. The cuts were a particular shame because they replaced the grisly fates of two characters in live action with still images and so greatly negated the impact of two segment endings. Thankfully, Vault of Horror can now be seen as it was intended.

The framing device in Vault of Horror is fun and the film begins with shots of the Houses Of Parliament and stirringly ominous music from Douglas Gamley. Right away we are back in the comfortingly kitsch and enjoyably spooky aura of Amicus anthology world. We pan across the water to a high-rise tower by the Thames and meet the cast one by one as they all enter a descending lift. You can't help laughing when you see they include aquatic James Bond supervillain Carl Stromberg from The Spy Who Loved Me (otherwise known as actor Curd Jürgens) and Tom Baker with one of the most ridiculous beards in cinematic history. It's a miracle really that Baker was actually able to fit the beard in the lift. They are joined by Michael Craig (looking uncannily like Des Lynam), Terry-Thomas and Daniel Massey.

These characters are slightly perplexed though when the lift takes them all the way down to the sub-basement and then shuts the door on them. As sub-basements go though this one seems very snazzy with marble floors and a big table and chairs. "Looks like some sort of a club," says Des Lynam, I mean Michael Craig, surveying the decanters of brandy and booze sitting on the table. As a claustrophobic I wouldn't personally be quite so sanguine about being trapped in a sub-basement, even one as plush as this, but they don't seem unduly bothered. To be fair it does look very roomy and lavish. If you HAVE to be trapped somewhere then there are certainly worse places than this. Like my cellar for instance. I wouldn't like to be trapped down there because it's full of junk and the light doesn't work. Anyway, that's enough about my cellar, let's get back to Vault of Horror.

Tom Baker suggests they might as well make the most of it so they all sit down and pour themselves a glass of something and begin to chat. They've all had very vivid dreams (or nightmares to be more precise) recently that seemed very real. "So very, very real," adds Terry-Thomas helpfully to the dream themed banter later on, just in case we hadn't got the gist. Daniel Massey is the first to share his own particular recurring nightmare and we are off and running.

The first segment is Midnight Mess * and stars Daniel Massey and his real life sister Anna. There is also a brief appearance by Mike Pratt of Randall and Hopkirk fame as a private investigator and Pratt surely deserved an award of some sort just for his seventies outfit (a brown leather jacket complimented by a gigantic and vivid red neck scarf). He also has a wild and not inconsiderable beard so Vault of Horror is a great film generally for fans of comedy beards.

Daniel Massey is (the wonderfully named) Harold Rogers, a thoroughly unpleasant chap in this story. He tracks down his sister (Anna Massey obviously) for sinister purposes to a strange town where there is talk of murders and warnings not to venture out at night. "Why is everyone afraid of the dark here?" asks Harold. "Because of them!" his sister replies in somewhat cryptic fashion. After getting up to all sorts of mischief, Harold decides to have some supper in a restaurant he spots open late at night. This is a very odd restaurant though, as he will discover for himself as the secrets of the town are slowly revealed...

Daniel Massey is great fun in Midnight Mess. He makes

Richard Hillman look like Basil Brush and is a very nasty piece of work. The atmosphere developed here is suitably strange and mysterious so that you want the segment to run for much longer than it does. The town Daniel Massey visits is very empty and he is perplexed when he first tries to enter the restaurant for a bite to eat only to be told it is closing because it will be dark soon. When he spies it open later he enters to find it has completely fresh staff. His dinner in the weird restaurant is an excellent scene ("Ah, tomato juice!") with a great revelation moment, all heightened by another of Douglas Gamley's spooky scores. You can argue that they might have been better in Vault of Horror dropping one of the weaker segments and allowing a few others, especially Midnight Mess, to be just a bit longer.

Midnight Mess has a fantastically EC Comics ending and Massey makes a fine villain. I must say though his evil antics are not very well thought through on his part. He murders his sister (despite the fact he's bound to be the prime suspect because he'll make money from her death) and then straight after the murder goes across the road to have dinner in a restaurant! Surely he's going to be very easy to catch isn't he? Jack the Ripper didn't murder his sister and then walk ten yards down the road and stop for pie and mash at an inn. That's why they never caught him! Midnight Mess is a great start to Vault of Horror and classic horror anthology fun.

Now onto the second segment - which is another classic. The Neat Job stars Terry-Thomas as a rather mature bachelor called Arthur Gritchit with a fondness for huge cravats and classical music. He lives in the most seventies bungalow ever put on film with extensive use of the colours brown and yellow. In fact, even his pots and pans are yellow. Gritchit's bachelor days are finally ended when he ties the knot with the somewhat clumsy Eleanor (Glynis Johns) and she moves into his garish seventies abode. It honestly wouldn't surprise you if you learned that Gritchit's interior decorator had been arrested and been forced to serve a short prison sentence. Tension soon arises because Gritchit is an obsessively tidy and neat person to the point of being slightly mad - as Eleanor soon discovers. But how much of this can Eleanor put up with before she goes mad too?

One of the highlights of Vault of Horror occurs for me when Terry-Thomas declares "What a smashing breakfast!" after Eleanor tries to make an effort to get in his good books one morning with some cooked grub. You wonder why she bothers though as this is a man who is driven potty by the slightest sign of disorder or untidiness. You can see why Arthur has been a bachelor for so long. He's set in his ways and sharing his house with someone is definitely not a good idea. Gritchit plainly has an extreme form of OCD. If you put a cup down in the wrong place he's liable to have a nervous breakdown.

Gritchit is quite an interesting villain because he is not innately evil like James Elliot in Tales from the Crypt or Harold Rogers in Midnight Mess. If anything, Arthur Gritchit is oblivious to the fact that he's being beastly and abusive to Eleanor and making her life a misery. His crimes are not the usual anthology horror crimes of lust, pursuit of money, or murder but merely the fact that he is selfish and unthinking. The novel thing about this segment is that, the memorable EC Comics style resolution aside, there is not really any traditional horror in it - apart perhaps from a moment when Gritchit accidentally puts a pair of Eleanor's pink knickers on in the morning because she's muddled the underwear drawers up.

The suspense comes from Eleanor desperately trying to tidy up as the clock ticks down to Gritchit arriving home from work, her desperation leading to an escalating series of accidents where she spills something on the carpet and makes a mess of his cellar workshop when she tries to find a nail to hang a picture back on the wall. This simple premise is surprisingly gripping. Glynis Johns, who died in 2024 at the age of 100 and had a truly amazing career, is great too in this segment as poor Eleanor, especially when she visibly shudders each time Terry-Thomas shouts "ELEANOR!!" after finding something out of place or his meticulous cupboards bereft of pasta sauce. The Neat Job is great fun, not least for the performance of Terry-Thomas as the fusspot with a 'tidy' fetish.

The next segment This Trick'll Kill You is a bit obvious and predictable but it's mildly interesting not least for the presence of one of my favourite Bond baddies in Curd Jürgens. Jurgens is Sebastian, a magician mooching around India (though it's obviously a series of sets) with his wife (Dawn Addams) looking for new tricks to perform in his act. Nothing much impresses this silver haired and morose Paul Daniels though until he watches an extraordinary performance of the Indian rope-trick and asks the girl who performed it to demonstrate the trick to him and his wife in his hotel room. Sebastian is unable to work out how the trick is done so decides to just half-inch the rope and do away with the Indian girl. As you'd expect in an Amicus compendium horror, this is not the smartest move in the world.

You can see where This Trick'll Kill is going a mile off and it's the weakest of the segments here because of its slow pace. It does have a relatively creepy ending though and Jürgens is on firm ground as the taciturn Sebastian. One slight problem here is that the story plays out in a series of all too obvious cheap sets and so the segment generally lacks any notable visual flourishes or interesting location work. Amicus obviously were not going to go to India to shoot a short segment for Vault of Horror! This Trick'll Kill You is the only segment in this film that I find a slight chore to sit through. It might actually have been more fun if the story was about a magician up to no good in Blighty. That way the segment would have more Amicus residue because these films tend to have very British backdrops.

"It begins in a graveyard... in a grave... a freshly dug grave... my grave... buried alive!" We move onto Bargain in Death with Michael Craig as Maitland, a horror writer with no money who drugs himself to appear dead and is buried alive as part of an insurance scam. "Even the best doctor will think that I'm dead," promises the confident rascal. But can he trust his partner in crime Alex (Edward Judd) to come and dig him out? Further complicating matters are medical students Robin Nedwell and Geoffrey Davies (though sadly no Richard O'Sullivan) from the Doctor sitcoms of the era who want to dig up a body to help with their studies and rope in Arthur Mullard as a gravedigger.

Bargain in Death is not bad but far from the best story on offer here. It has a decentish premise and a grisly ending but the presence of the sitcom stars (who look a bit old to be medical students if you ask me - Geoffrey Davies clearly has some grey hair!) and Arthur Mullard seems a trifle incongruous and tacked on, as if Amicus were determined to get a few more guest stars into the mix. The tone is consequently rather inconsistent and the comic antics of Nedwell and Davies negates the creepiness potential of all the graveyard shenanigans. There is a great in-joke here though when we see Maitland, waiting for the effects of the heart slowing drugs to kick in and make him appear dead, reading a novelisation of the previous Amicus anthology film Tales From the Crypt. "There is no money in horror," sighs Maitland on his financial troubles!

Vault Of Horror ends on a high with Drawn and Quartered starring the bonkers Tom Baker as a bearded artist named Moore with big hair living in a bamboo hut in Haiti. Moore, suffering from a creative malaise, visits a local exponent of voodoo and is granted some of its power. Whatever he draws or paints will now happen. If he draws a scar on his cheek then something will happen to give him a scar on his cheek. If he draws a picture of someone and destroys the picture that person will be killed in real life etc.

This new talent comes in handy when Moore discovers a bunch of poncy art people in London have been ripping him off, making money from paintings they told him were worthless. Moore is tipped off to the fact that his paintings are now going for some real cash in Blighty by an old friend who just happens to pop around to his bamboo hut in Haiti to say hello, as you do. I just nipped out and suddenly decided to do the shopping in Haiti today and I heard you were in the area so I thought I'd drop in! Our impoverished artist decides to head home to extract a suitable revenge with his new voodoo super powers.

Drawn and Quartered is a funny and entertaining segment with Baker and the hokey Haitian 'locations'. Baker's scenes in Haiti are not terribly authentic but it's all part of the fun really. He is in Haiti in the sense that the cast of Carry On Up the

Jungle were in Africa or the cast of It Ain't Half Hot Mum were in Burma. I could go on but you get the general idea. There is actually some real location work in London that is quite good fun though. Amicus had contemporary settings to save money but now that these compendiums are period pieces themselves it all adds to the charm.

The device here of images altered on his canvas then happening in real life is an effective one and daft voodoo capers are an Amicus tradition. The voodoo painting possibilities are endless but this being a short and modestly budgeted segment in an Amicus anthology he uses them strictly for revenge on a selection of dubious characters. You'd think he would have done at least a couple of strange things purely out of curiosity. A giant squid attacking the House of Commons or make it rain custard creams. There's a classic moment in this segment though when when the baddies has a grisly accident with a paper cutter! Drawn and Quartered also features a wonderfully smug and nasty turn by Denholm Elliot and is always fun with quite a tense resolution. You can't really go wrong with Tom Baker in a giant beard and seventies outfits. Drawn and Quartered never fails to entertain me and make me laugh.

Vault of Horror is very enjoyable on the whole and stacks up reasonably well against the other Amicus compendiums. Midnight Mess, The Neat Job and Drawn and Quartered are really good in particular with This Trick'll Kill You and Bargain in Death not quite so memorable. Anyone who loves these Amicus anthologies should enjoy this a lot although I think Tales From the Crypt is slightly better, Vault of Horror essentially being an unofficial sequel to that film. Obviously Vault of Horror is not Lawrence of Arabia and looks slightly muddy and dated at times but, with an effective score by Douglas Gamley, this is tremendous fun at times and a must for anyone with a sweet tooth for British horror films - especially camp seventies portmanteau ones with lots of famous faces.

Just a word too about the framing sequence in this film, which is often cited as being unimaginative and forgettable. Well, what's wrong with having these characters in a slightly surreal looking basement gentlemen's club room around a huge table? I think it works fine. As to questions like, why don't they look for a way out?, well, the ending of the film, as I need hardly explain, answers that one. I find the ending of this film effectively haunting and dreamlike - or nightmare-like if you prefer!

* Midnight Mess is another story that was remade for the HBO series Tales from the Crypt in the 1990s. In the HBO show it was called Mournin' Mess and directed by Manny Coto. Have no fear of repetition if you are an Amicus fan because this version is very different and more faithful to the EC comic. Dale Sweeney (Steven Weber) is a crooked reporter and all round rake who is a bit down of his luck. He soon becomes drawn into a couple of big stories though and may wish he hadn't in the end. Homeless people are being murdered and a wealthy organisation named the Grateful Homeless Outcasts and Unwanteds Layaway Society (just think about that name) has popped up, offering a dignified and proper burial for deceased homeless people who had no one to arrange a service for them. Sweeney investigates these twin stories and begins to unearth a very big secret. Mournin' Mess is well directed with a pulpy feel and an underlying sense of unease and the final reveal is very Tales from the Crypt. The distinctive looking Vincent Schiavelli is great in his scenes as a homeless man who tips Sweeney off about the case and Rita Wilson is well cast too as Jess Gilchrist, the main PR honcho for the mysterious charitable organisation. The last scene in Mournin' Mess is rather scary I think.

AND NOW THE SCREAMING STARTS! (1973)

And Now the Screaming Starts! was directed by Roy Ward Baker and written by Roger Marshall. It is is based on the 1970 novella Fengriffen by David Case. The film version was called

Ferngriffen too through its production but then changed for the release. The cast were said to be rather annoyed when they saw that this Fengriffen film they'd worked on was now called And Now the Screaming Starts! If we know one thing about Max Rosenberg and Milton Subotsky by now it's that they did love their crazy eye-catching film titles.

Max Rosenberg (cheekily) wanted to call this film I Have No Mouth and I Must Scream but Harlan Ellison nipped that in the bud by taking legal action.

This is the only Amicus film that Stephanie Beacham made - which is a shame. She had just appeared in the campy and enjoyable Hammer film Dracula A.D. 1972. The year before that she was in The Nightcomers with Marlon Brando. The Nightcomers is a prequel to Henry James' 1898 novella The Turn of the Screw and was directed by Michael Winner. Stephanie Beacham certainly did the rounds when it came to the British horror industry. She was in two Pete Walker films (House of Mortal Sin and Schizo) and also Norman J. Warren's Inseminoid in 1981. Inseminoid is often dubbed an Alien copycat although the makers insisted it was written before Alien came out. The key difference is that Alien is an expensive and well made film while Inseminoid was shot in three weeks in some caves in Kent! As with Joan Collins, Stephanie ended up in the American soap opera Dynasty. She was in the spin-off show the Colbys at first before joining the base show.

Ian Ogilvy was already no stranger to horror films having appeared in The She Beast, The Sorcerers, and Witchfinder General for the late Michael Reeves. He would become best known for playing Simon Templar on television in Return of the Saint. In his later years Ogilvy did a lot of American television. Ian Ogilvy (who was very dashing in his youth - and still quite dashing today) was frequently mentioned as a James Bond candidate in the 1970s and 1980s but he obviously never bagged that famous part. Ogilvy said that, purely by chance, he later once found himself having lunch with Jerry Juroe - who the head of publicity for the James Bond production company EON. Juroe told Ian Ogilvy that the reason why they never cast him as James Bond is that he was deemed too similar to Roger

Moore!

Anyway, what is the plot of Fengriffen, sorry, I mean And Now the Screaming Starts! Set in 1795, Catherine (Stephanie Beacham) has married the wealthy baron Charles Fengriffen (Ian Ogilvy) and moved into his grand country mansion. Married bliss awaits. But not so fast. Something supernatural abounds in this large gothic house. Catherine is attacked by some sort of malevolent spirit and falls pregnant. A family curse seems to reside in these parts and it all seems to revolve around the mysterious estate woodsman Silas (Geoffrey Whitehead).

This film is one of the few times when Amicus seemed intent on - for all intents and purposes - making a Hammer picture. If you had no knowledge of And Now the Screaming Starts! and skipped the credits at the start you would almost certainly presume it was a Hammer production you were watching. In a way it was almost like an in-joke by Amicus. Hammer were now experimenting with films set in the present day like Dracula A.D 1972 so what better time for Amicus to take a lunch break from their modern day anthologies and make a gothic period caper?

Luckily for Amicus, And Now the Screaming Starts! is fairly solid on most levels. This is one of the better films they produced away from the anthology format. The production here is very competent and has the steady (if unspectacular) fingerprints of the reliable Roy Ward Baker all over it. There is nothing spectacular on offer here but it's just a solid mystery that is competent on most levels and always very watchable.

In many ways, And Now the Screaming Starts! reminds me of Hammer's excellent Hound of the Baskervilles adaptation - and not only because Peter Cushing arrives to take over in the second act of both pictures. Both films have a rich period atmosphere and make good use of colour and fog bound woods. They also both have a fun flashback sequence that highlights the dastardly deeds of a wicked ancestor.

A big factor in the atmosphere of And Now the Screaming Starts! is the use of Oakley Court, a Victorian Gothic country house set in 35 acres overlooking the River Thames at Water Oakley in Berkshire. Oakley Court has been used for many horror films over the years. The Brides of Dracula, The Reptile, The Plague of the Zombies, and Mumsy, Nanny, Sonny, and Girly to name but a few.

The costumes and sets in And Now the Screaming Starts! are very good and Stephanie Beacham's corset cleavage almost deserves to have its own credit. Beacham justifies her reputation here as one of the most reliable scream queens of the era. She works especially well during her scenes with Cushing - a consequence presumably of them having acted together before. What really makes this film a treat though is the presence of Amicus veterans Patrick Magee and Cushing. Magee plays the family doctor - a man who clearly knows more than he is letting on. Magee is magnetic in his usual quiet eccentric way. Even watching Magee sit in a chair or sip a drink is strangely compelling.

Cushing is Dr Pope, a psychiatrist of sorts and apparently someone greatly interested in legends and folklore. Pope is called in by Ogilvy's character to see if he can treat Catherine. Cushing more or less becomes the main character from here on in as he investigates the mystery. He gives - as ever - an impeccable and thoroughly committed performance. Cushing brings some real energy to this part and his costume (complete with foppish wig) in particular is a lot of fun. As if all this wasn't enough you also get Herbert Lom as an evil ancestor of Fengriffen. Lom is tremendously over the top in his usual way but it's always a pleasure to watch Herbert Lom chew some scenery up.

The only cast member who gets short shrift here is probably Ian Ogilvy. Ogilvy doesn't get much to do, especially in the first half of the film. He mostly appears worried and hovvers in a few corridors. Later on they give him a few more 'actiony' bits when he confronts the woodsman and takes an axe to a grave. Having said that though, Lom is in the film for about ten minutes and Peter Cushing is in less than half the film's running time. I suspect Amicus did that old trick of not hiring the bigger names for very long to keep costs down. I should mention Geoffrey Whitehead too, who is appropriately enigmatic and sinister as Silas.

And Now the Screaming Starts! is agreeable enough on the

whole. There's a great cast, a fine period atmosphere, and a few twists and turns. I think the story might be a trifle on the slow side for some tastes but it's always very watchable and the music cues by Douglas Gamley add a familiar and distinctive Amicus backdrop to the gothic capers onscreen. This is a very competent film and a perfectly acceptable and decent attempt by Amicus to make the sort of horror film that you'd associate more with their illustrious and legendary rivals Hammer.

FROM BEYOND THE GRAVE (1974)

From Beyond the Grave sadly turned out to be the last of the Amicus anthology films and so marked the end of an era. It was originally titled The Undead and is also known as The Creatures, Tales from Beyond the Grave, and Tales from the Beyond. Some fresh (ahem) blood was brought in for this last anthology, most notably Kevin Connor, who gained his first directing credit here. Connor would go to helm the Amicus ahistorical family adventure caper films The Land That Time Forgot, At the Earth's Core and The People That Time Forgot with Doug McClure in the same decade. The cinematographer Alan Hume (who would later work on both the Star Wars and James Bond franchises) worked well with Connor to give From Beyond the Grave an inventive look.

How did Connor get the job? "In the early 70's I optioned a dozen short stories from Chetwynd Hayes entitled The Unbidden thinking to make a TV series out of them. Myself and two friends adapted them into half hour films and unsuccessfully shopped them around the TV world. Somehow they landed on Milton's desk and he called me in to chat about them. The upshot was that he selected 4 of them and wrote a connecting story (the Peter Cushing link) and offered me the directing task. After I picked myself up off the floor and told him that I had never directed a whole film – he uttered the immortal words editors make good directors and I'll surround you with great actors and technicians. He did and that's how Beyond The Grave came about and my career started."

Ronald Chetwynd-Hayes (1917-2001) was a British author and editor, best known for his horror and fantasy fiction. He was born in London and attended King's College School before studying at the Royal Academy of Dramatic Art. Chetwynd-Hayes worked as an actor for several years before turning to writing. Chetwynd-Hayes became a prolific writer of horror and supernatural fiction in the 1960s and 1970s. His stories often featured traditional horror elements such as vampires, ghosts, and werewolves, but he also infused humour into his work, earning him the nickname The Prince of Chill. In addition to his writing, Chetwynd-Hayes also edited several horror anthologies, including the Fontana Book of Great Horror Stories series. He was known for discovering and promoting new talent in the genre, and many of his anthologies featured stories from up-and-coming authors. Chetwynd-Hayes' work gained a cult following, and he became an influential figure in the British horror scene.

Max Rosenberg later said that Amicus thought the anthology horror film goose was cooked by this point and they planned to move on to other things but Warner Bros persuaded them to do another anthology film. However, when they viewed From Beyond the Grave, Warner Bros hated the film and so Amicus got the rights back. I don't know what Warner Bros were expecting because From Beyond the Grave supplies exactly what you'd expect of an Amicus anthology film! It could be the case that Warners were expecting something a bit more modern or cutting edge. I don't really know. The horror landscape was changing fast by 1974. That year saw the release of films like The Texas Chainsaw Massacre, Black Christmas, and House of Whipcord. The previous year saw the release of The Exorcist.

Peter Cushing returned for From Beyond the Grave in one his best roles in the Amicus films and joining him was another interesting and varied Amicus cast. The always entertaining Donald Pleasence and Ian Bannen, up and comers Ian Ogilvy, the brilliant David Warner (who would go on to be in literally everything from Star Trek to The Omen to Time Bandits), and

Lesley-Anne Down, and, in the Amicus tradition, a few names who had seen better days in Ian Carmichael, Margaret Leighton and the great Diana Dors. The beautiful Lesley-Anne Down would go on to appear in films like The Pink Panther Strikes Again and The First Great Train Robbery. When her film career faded she later did a lot of American television. I don't think Lesley-Anne would thank me for this but I always remember her for Death Wish V: The Face of Death!

In her youth Diana Dors was regarded to be Britain's version of Marilyn Monroe and under contract to film studios in both Britain and the United States. She was symbolic of a post-war yearning for glamour and flaunted her money and 'blonde bombshell' looks and figure. The young Diana Dors would have been a tabloid fixture to rival anyone today with her marriages, affairs (everyone from Rod Steiger to Bob Monkhouse), her powder-blue Cadillac, wild parties, and the criminal connections of some of the men who passed through her colourful life.

Dors was born Diana Fluck (yes, you can see why she had to change her name) in Swindon in 1931. She studied at the London Academy of Music and Dramatic Art and appeared in films for Rank, later coming under contract to RKO and moving to Hollywood. Despite the Monroe tag the closer parallel is probably Jayne Mansfield who, like Dors, sort of created a character to play. Diana Dors was a much better actor than Mansfied though. When Dors lived in Hollywood, numerous famous names (Doris Day, Debbie Reynolds etc) were guests at swanky parties at her house but Dors soon began to stretch the patience of RKO. Her first husband Denis Hamilton beat her 'black and blue' according to a biographer and would turn down film roles on her behalf without telling her.

Hamilton wrecked Diana's Hollywood career by kicking a photographer in the head during an infamous pool party incident. Offers to work with Robert Mitchum and Jerry Lewis vanished and she was effectively blackballed in Hollywood, considered too much trouble, prone to affairs and wayward behaviour. It's actually quite difficult at times to keep up with the full tumult of Diana Dors life - which took in three marriages, dozens of affairs and lovers, abortion, custody battles over children, debt, bankruptcy, media gossip and battles with illness until her premature death at the age of 52.

Dors' early notoriety stemmed from stories fed to the press by Hamilton. Her exploits and dress sense would seem rather tame today but it was cheeky stuff back then. In 1960 she was criticised by the archbishop of Canterbury Dr Geoffrey Fisher for being a bad role model after some of her memoirs were published in a newspaper! At the height of her fame, Dors was turning down Bob Hope films because she didn't want to dye her hair, having an affair with Rod Steiger, appearing on US chat shows and living in a villa off Sunset Boulevard. She even brought out a couple of records and appeared on the Beatles' Sgt Pepper's Lonely Hearts Club Band album cover.

Her looks though were inevitably not going to last forever The film roles were drying up and Dors had started to put weight on. Britain's answer to Marilyn Monroe would end up being cast as the nagging dowdy wife in low-budget seventies comedy and horror films. The Inland Revenue went after her for £40,000 in the sixties. Her reaction to a tax bill that she knew would wipe her out was to throw a fireworks party and practically burn her house down in the process! Dors was notorious for hosting 'sex parties' and drugs were apparently rife in her home. She retained a warm image though and was a beloved British institution in her last years and a fixture on breakfast television.

A lot of people rank From Beyond the Grave as the best of the Amicus anthology films and you could plausibly make a case for that. I find the previous three a trifle more entertaining on the whole but From Beyond the Grave is still very enjoyable and certainly on the same sort of par. This is probably the best looking of the Amicus anthology films and surprisingly inventive and classy in places. The cast is amazing too. It seems very fitting for Peter Cushing to be at the heart of this last Amicus anthology as the star of the wraparound and he seems to be enjoying himself as the eccentric owner of the little antiques shop. It's a slight shame though that Christopher Lee doesn't feature in the film. Lee was absent for the last four Amicus anthologies.

The start of the film is wonderfully atmospheric as we swoop through Highgate Cemetary. The framing device in From Beyond the Grave, always a fun component of these films, has Peter Cushing as the enigmatic old owner of Temptations Ltd, a dusty antiques shop (motto: Offers You Cannot Resist) in a small, anachronistic backstreet. Cushing, with flat cap, pipe and Northern accent, promises a surprise with every purchase. This is certainly the case for those customers who attempt to cheat him out of some money or half-inch something because this antiques shop is not all that it seems.

The end of the titles flow straight from the cemetery to the street where the antiques shop sits. The visual clue is obvious. Don't be fooled by the kindly owner. There is something of the night about this shop. However, Cushing's proprietor does have a moral compass. If you play fair with him then nothing will happen to you. It seems possible that From Beyond the Grave might have been a vague influence on the Stephen King story Needful Things. Needful Things revolves around a mysterious curiosity shop and explores themes of greed and temptation.

The first story is called The Gatecrasher and features David Warner and some extraordinary shirts as Edward Charlton. The somewhat smug Edward makes a big mistake when he swindles Cushing out of some money in Temptations Ltd by pretending he's spotted that an antique mirror is a reproduction and attaining this item at a bargain price. Once back in his groovy bachelor pad Edward gradually realises that there is something very strange about this mirror after his friends badger him into holding a seance. In fact, the mirror may contain the spirit of a very nasty character indeed and he's eager to make his presence felt...

The Gatecrasher is an atmospheric and enjoyable segment which feels inspired by similar spooky mirror shenanigans with Googie Withers and Ralph Michael in the 1945 Ealing classic Dead of Night. Weird fog and strange faces appearing in mirrors are always quite creepy and this episode is very enjoyable on the whole as Edward's life is slowly turned upside down. The direction is quite good in this one too with

Warner's dodgy flat antics and neighbours wondering what is going on reminding me of that classic Hitchcock film Frenzy a little at times and I love the spooky seance with candlelight and the camera panning past the faces of Edward's friends.

There is a nice inventive sequence too in The Gatecrasher where the passage of time is highlighted by a quick montage of the flat and its changing decor and residents. Kevin Connor's helming of this segment and the editing is very good. Another plus is the presence of David Warner, an actor who was always good value and fully committed to whatever nonsense his agent has put him in. There is a nice final twist also in The Gatecrasher which wraps things up very neatly in suitably spooky fashion.

The second story is called An Act of Kindness and features Ian Bannen as Christopher Lowe, a timid and henpecked husband stuck in a boring office job and married to Mabel, played by Diana Dors in full late career battleaxe mode. Considered a joke at home by Mabel and his son, Lowe befriends threadbare matchbox and shoelace street vendor and old soldier Jim Underwood (Donald Pleasance) who he passes by on the way to and from work. Lowe comes to enjoy the fact that Jim salutes him and calls him Sir, affording him the respect he never gets at home.

Browsing in Temptations Ltd, Lowe tries to buy a Distinguished Service Medal to impress the old soldier Jim. But Cushing's crusty old shop owner wants the certificate to prove Lowe really was with Monty's Eighth Army in North Africa as he claims and a decorated war hero. Lowe doesn't have such a certificate so he steals the medal instead when the owner's back is turned. Impressed by the medal, Jim invites Lowe to his home for some tea where he is soon a regular guest and involved in a relationship with Jim's rather creepy young daughter Emily (Angela Pleasence).

An Act of Kindness is another good segment featuring a wonderfully uptight performance by Ian Bannen as the frustrated Lowe. His dinner table scenes with Diana Dors are very funny as Dors slams his dinner on the table and generally lets him know she thinks he's a complete idiot. Another plus is of course Donald Pleasence as the deferential old soldier. The thing that makes this segment work, in addition to the enjoyable cast, is the nature of the mystery that unravels. You genuinely have no idea what is going to unfold and why Jim is being so kind and generous to Lowe beyond the fact that he claims to have been in the army. Angela Pleasence is well cast too as Jim's rather odd and mysterious daughter.

The third story lightens the tone slightly and is called The Elemental. It features Ian Carmichael as Reggie Warren, a very posh bowler hat and umbrella businessman. The pompous Reggie makes a big mistake when he assumes Cushing's antiques proprietor is a doddering old fossil who can barely remember his own name and switches some price tags in Temptations Ltd to get an antique snuff box on the cheap. "I hope you enjoy snuffing it," says Cushing.

On the way home in the train Reggie is bothered in his compartment by an annoying and rather theatrical woman called Madame Orloff (Margaret Leighton), a professional psychic who tells him he has an 'Elemental' on his shoulder. Reggie of course assumes this woman is mad and goes back to his paper to see what the Test Match score is or something but once home in his unfeasibly gigantic country house with wife Susan (Nyree Dawn Porter) strange things soon start to happen.

The Elemental is often a more frivolous tale than the first two with comic elements but becomes scarier as it goes on and the idea of an invisible demon/ghost sitting on your shoulder is quite a creepy one. Ian Carmichael is fun as the disconcertingly upper-class commuter with a house like an embassy and Margaret Leighton chews up the scenery and spits it out with a ridiculously broad and over the top performance as Madame Orloff that skirts past flamboyant and enters the realm of completely bonkers. This is not my favourite segment on offer here but not bad and not without its charms.

The final story is called The Door and stars a suave young Ian Ogilvy as William Seaton. Seaton purchases an ancient ornate door from Temptations Ltd - although we are not quite allowed to see if he ripped off Peter Cushing's spooky Lovejoy or not. Once home Seaton and lovely wife Rosemary (Lesley-

Anne Down) find themselves becoming entranced by the door and although they've used it as the entrance to their stationary cupboard, it seems to sometimes open into a very mysterious blue room rather than, you know, shelves of pencils and, er, rulers and things.

The Door is a decent (though very brief) segment although not that scary and lacking the theatrical blood that occasionally flows in some of the other stories. The design is quite atmospheric though and it looks great at times. This is a fairly decent - if straightforward - ghostly tale with occult trappings and Ogilvy is earnest enough as the haunted door capers escalate. Jack Watson pops up in this one as a historical villain of an occult bent. What is interesting about this segment is that it has a twist at the end when it comes to the cosmic karma and people getting a deserved comeuppance in these anthology films. As we've mentioned before, the trick to surviving an Amicus anthology horror film is to be a nice person. It doesn't cost anything to be nice and considerate of others. If you are a kind decent person then you won't end up in the catacombs or a sub-basement in Millbank Tower. And if you don't steal anything from Temptations Ltd you won't get a nasty surprise.

We then go back to Pctcr Cushing and the antiques shop one more time for an enjoyable end to the film. "The love of money is the root of all evil," he laments sadly.

From Beyond the Grave is a lot of fun overall. The film is well directed and you are kept guessing here and there as to how these tales will resolve themselves. The cast is great, especially Cushing - who is wonderful as the bushy eyebrowed shop owner. I particularly like his little looks and comments to himself when some shady looking character takes a browse in his shop. "Naughty, shouldn't have done that." Most of all though, From Beyond the Grave presents more slightly camp and very British seventies compendium horror antics in the best Amicus tradition. It's a shame really that this was the last anthology hurrah.

Given that this was the last anthology film and Amicus didn't last for that much longer, you might expect From Beyond the Grave to have a slightly tired feel and the law of diminishing returns to be at play. That isn't the case at all though. The new director helps to freshen the formula up and give the film some arresting visual flourishes and on the evidence of this anthology Amicus could have easily made a couple more. Amicus decided in the end though to move away from horror and go back to family adventure films. They evidently made a calculation that anthology horror films were old hat - or at least not making enough money. What a legacy they left though when it comes to anthology horror films. No one quite did it quite like Amicus. Take those V/H/S found footage horror anthology films they churn out today. Would you rather watch one of those again or Tales from the Crypt or Asylum again? It's no contest really is it?

MADHOUSE (1974)

Madhouse was directed by Jim Clark and written by Ken Levison and Greg Morrison. It was based on the book Devilday by Angus Hall. The working title of the film was The Revenge of Dr Death. Jim Clark didn't direct many films but he was an acclaimed editor on many others - including The Killing Fields and The Innocents. This was a co-production between Amicus and American International Pictures. You get AIP legend Vincent Price heading up the cast and he's joined by Amicus and Hammer legend Peter Cushing. As if that wasn't enough you also get Count Yorga himself Robert Quarry.

Vincent Price was an art collector, a gourmet chef, an expert gardener with an incredible cymbidium orchid collection, an author, a lover of museums and galleries, and a more distinguished actor than his more high camp horror duties would sometimes allow, once winning raves for a one man show about Oscar Wilde. In two of his very last films, The Whales of August and Edward Scissorhands, he showed there was a lot more to his acting than chewing the scenery up in a dungeon somewhere.

Price was born in St Louis in 1911 into a fairly well to do

family. He was rather anti-Semitic in his youth but this was apparently a common failing of people of that time from his class and he later became a supporter of the Jewish Anti-Defamation League. He was married to Mary Grant Price and Coral Browne. Price had a good sense of humour that was sometimes slightly macabre. He loved to take his daughter Victoria trick or treating at Halloween in particular. Imagine opening the door on Halloween night and finding Vincent Price on your doorstep! He also apparently had a tremendous love of roller-coasters!

Victoria remembers visiting him in England when he was shooting Theatre of Blood. Price was Edward Lionheart, a vain actor who fakes his death and murders snooty theatrical critics in Shakespearean fashion. She says they visited the small theatre set where Price was filming and were surrounded by shuffling tramps, milling about like zombies. These were of course merely extras playing Lionheart's underground cult and a practical joke on the part of her father.

Despite his spooky presence in any number of spooky films (and a few television and radio shows too), Price was a fairly gentle character in real life and loved nothing more than pottering about in the kitchen or garden or watching documentaries on television. Price loved the sea and was at his most content and happy when they went fishing or spent hours walking along the beach looking for driftwood and stones to skim across the water. Although he was an exceptionally intelligent and refined man, Price didn't begrudge the fact that tongue-in-cheek (and sometimes not so tongue-in-cheek) performances in horror films of varying degrees of quality became his stock in trade. He was happy for the work and grateful for the boost they gave to his profile but he did privately admit that some of these films were pretty silly at times.

Linda Hayden, who briefly plays Elizabeth Peters in Madhouse, was already a bit of a horror veteran despite only being about 21 when this film came out. Hayden shot to fame in the 1969 film Baby Love - a film which helped resurrect the flagging career of Diana Dors. Linda Hayden's film career sadly went south in the end. She was in a couple of

Confessions films, the 'video nasty' Exposé, and - worst of all - Queen Kong with Robin Askwith. Queen Kong is a British comedy spoof of King Kong and a very obscure film. The producer Dino De Laurentiis took legal action against the film when it tried to ride the coat tails of his own big budget King Kong remake. He shouldn't have bothered really. Queen Kong was unseen for many years - which I'm sure the cast were relieved about. Well, I HAVE seen Queen Kong. All I can say is that it makes Digby: The Biggest Dog in the World look like 2001: A Space Odyssey. Linda did have better luck on television - appearing in some good stuff like Hammer House of Mystery & Suspense and Minder On the Orient Express.

In the plot of Madhouse, Vincent Price plays Robert Toombes. Toombes is a veteran horror actor famous for his long running film role as 'Dr Death' - a sinister horror villain who wears a skull like mask. Tombes is about to marry Ellen Mason (Julie Crosthwait) but is irritated at the engagement party by a crass producer named Oliver Quayle (Robert Quarry) - who is well out of order if you ask me. Quayle reminds Toombes that Ellen used to make 'adult' films for him. That's certainly one way of putting a dampener on one's engagement party!

Ellen is upset by the reaction of Toombes to this most unwelcome reminder of her past. She tearfully goes to her room but a man dressed as Dr Death appears. When Toombs goes up to apologise to Ellen he finds she has been murdered. Decapitated no less. Toombes spends some time in a mental institution and is not even sure himself if he killed Ellen or not. Years later, Toombes is asked to go to England where his old friend Herbert Flay (Peter Cushing) has done a deal to make a Dr Death television series with Oliver Quayle producing. However, as soon as Toombes arrives murders start abounding. Could the culprit really be Dr Death?

Madhouse has some flaws but it is a very interesting film that offers plenty of Amicus fun. It was made on the cusp of that period when Hammer and Amicus were starting to look anachronistic and the horror genre was changing. 1974 was the year of The Texas Chainsaw Massacre lest we forget. Interestingly, it was also the year of Black Christmas *, the film often credited with starting the 'slasher' genre. Well, one could argue that Madhouse is also an early 'slasher' of sorts too. Look at the skull mask and flowing black cape of Dr Death. That's the same costume as the killer from Wes Craven's Scream series!

The fact that Dr Death is a famous beloved horror villain in Madhouse almost seems to anticipate the likes of Scream's masked killer, Jason, Michael Myers, Freddy, and the rest.

We didn't really, unless you count Hammer's Dracula films, have neverending horror franchises in 1974 - that was still to come with things like Halloween and Friday the 13th spinning out into many sequels - but the fact that Dr Death apparently featured in a long running franchise of his own and is being resurrected years later accurately predicts the future of horror.

Early on, you think Madhouse is going to be similar to Theatre of Blood or the Dr Phibes films, but it does confound your expectations in the end. Price plays a slightly unusual sort of character here as Toombs is gentle and vulnerable. You might even say that Price is often playing himself in this film. We have no idea if Toombs is a killer or not for most of Madhouse. Price is not really playing a Dr Phibes type character. The deaths are quite sparing and never very nasty. One might actually argue that there aren't enough of them. Madhouse is quite light on gore and mayhem.

There's a lot of meta commentary about the film industry and the changing nature of horror. Amusingly, we see Price and Cushing dressed as Dracula at one point - something which Cushing never got to do in the Hammer films. As you would imagine, any scene in the film that pairs Cushing and Price is a delight although - sadly - they are parted for the middle portion of the story. Toombs watches a lot of his old films in Madhouse and the films we see are actually old AIP Vincent Price pictures (most of the footage comes from the enjoyable anthology film Tales of Terror). While this device is effective and gives the character a bittersweet aura as he looks back at his past glories from yesteryear, it is perhaps a trifle overdone in the end, to the point where the old clips occasionally feel like padding. Madhouse is not a long film (it runs to about 90 minutes) but it still feels like it could lose ten minutes.

Robert Quarry, who ended up making endless Fred Olen Ray films when his career dipped, was always an enjoyable presence in horror films. There is a lot of stuff about how Quarry and Vincent Price hated each other and were rivals because Quarry was groomed at one point to replace Price as the main horror star at AIP. I've no idea if any of this is true but they did previously star in the Dr Phibes sequel together and the producer of that film said they got on fine and he never saw evidence of a rift or rivalry between them. It could be that this alleged rivalry was embellished in the media.

The director Jim Clark, who was a famous film editor, deploys some entertaining tricks throughout Madhouse with plenty of shots zooming down someone's cakehole as they start screaming! The supporting cast is good too - especially Adrienne Corri as Faye Carstairs, one of Toombes' former leads and now seemingly the captive of Flay. She's gone mad after suffering injuries in a car crash and lives in the cellar with a menagerie of spiders. The big flaw of Madhouse - if you want to be pedantic - is the fact that it's fairly obvious early on to deduce who is responsible for the murders. Consequently, there isn't a great amount of suspense.

This quibble aside (and the fact there could have been more death and horror), Madhouse is an interesting and well directed film. Price and Cushing are a joy in their scenes together and Price's big theatrical soliloquy near the end is worth the price of admission on its own. "Now I must play the final scene, the death of Dr Death!" Douglas Gamley's music cues are a perfect backdrop to the intrigue and there's a nice mix too of dark gothic candlelit houses and 'modern' parties and studio sequences on the set of Dr Death. No lesser figure than Michael Parkinson himself even has a cameo when Toombes appears on a chatshow. Madhouse is not perfect but it is a lot of fun and the pairing of Price and Cushing makes it one not to miss for any Amicus or horror fan.

* Black Christmas is a horror film directed by Bob Clark. It was made on a low-budget in Canada and got very sniffy reviews when it first came out. These days though Black Christmas is

considered to be a cult classic and a pivotal film in the horror genre. This was one of the first examples of the 'slasher' film and hugely influential. John Carpenter's Halloween was largely inspired by Black Christmas. The film takes place in a college sorority house just before Christmas. The girls in the house are being plagued by strange phone calls by a 'heavy breather'. The mysterious caller eventually threatens to kill them and, this being a horror film, they should probably take his warnings seriously. This film has a fantastic Christmas atmosphere but uses the festive trappings to be sinister rather than magical.

The weird phone calls are alarmingly creepy and Black Christmas is a pretty decent thriller in that there are a few red herrings and some misdirection. This film is certainly creepy but it isn't caked in blood or that gruesome at all. It's more about suspense than nasty kills or blood and guts. There's a decent enough cast here despite the low-budget of the film. Margot Kidder, about four years before she was cast as Lois Lane in the Superman movie with Christopher Reeve, has plenty of sass and charisma as Barb and Olivia Hussey is the nominal lead as Jess. There is also the ever dependable John Saxon as Lt. Fuller. Black Christmas is wonderfully effective in what it sets out to do and stacks up very well against the slew of stalker/slasher films which followed in its wake. It's rather perplexing to be honest that the film didn't get much acclaim when it first came out. The constrictive setting also works to the advantage of the film. if you are looking for something spooky to watch on Christmas Eve then Black Christmas is certainly recommended if you've never seen it before.

THE BEAST MUST DIE (1974)

The Beast Must Die is a somewhat camp (at the very least it teeters on the brink in unsteady fashion) horror film directed by Paul Annett and based on James Blish's story There Shall Be No Darkness. The screenplay was written by Michael Winder. Paul Annett mostly directed on television during his career. He directed 90 episodes of EastEnders. Among the other shows he directed on were The Adventures of Sherlock Holmes and Hammer House of Mystery & Suspense. He was the father of actress Chloë Annett - who took over as Kochanski from Claire Grogan in Red Dwarf.

Paul Annett said he hated the famous 'Werewolf Break' gimmick in The Beast Must Die because it made, in his words, the film 'stop dead'. I quite like it myself. Paul Annett said this gimmick was the idea of Milton Subotsky. The Beast Must Die is the only werewolf film that Amicus made. By a quirk of coincidence, Hammer only made one werewolf film too. The Beast Must Die was made at Shepperton and in and around the village of Pyrford in Surrey.

Robert Quarry was supposed to play the lead in this film but the producers replaced him with Calvin Lockhart due to the popularity of the blaxploitation films at the time. Calvin Lockhart was from the Bahamas and moved to New York as a teenager - where he took up acting. He was a stage actor and also appeared in films like Cotton Comes to Harlem, Uptown Saturday Night, Wild at Heart and Twin Peaks: Fire Walk with Me. Calvin also had a memorable death in Predator 2!

Amicus regular Peter Cushing was also signed up for The Beast Must Die. Marlene Clark, who play Lockhart's wife in the film, had been in films like Enter the Dragon and Beware the Blob. She would later become best known to American audiences for her part as Janet Lawson in the sitcom Sanford and Son. Oddly, Marlene Clark was dubbed by Annie Ross in The Beast Must Die. Annie Ross played Vera in Superman III. This was the woman who gets turned into an android by the super computer! Charles Gray had appeared in many films before The Beast Must Die - including two Bond films. He played Blofeld in Diamonds Are Forever and Henderson in You Only Live Twice. Shortly after The Beast Must Die, Gray featured in The Rocky Horror Show. I always remember Charles Gray the most for playing Mycroft in the enjoyable Sherlock Holmes series with Jeremy Brett.

Anton Diffring, who plays Lockhart's assistant in the film, was a German born actor who made a good living playing Nazis and German officers in war films. Diffring's father was

Jewish but some somehow managed to survive life in Nazi Germany. Anton Diffring made his way to England shortly before the war and eventually became a prolific actor. Michael Gambon was about 32 when he made The Beast Must Die. He would go onto to become one of the most acclaimed actors around. Unavoidably best known in the end for the Harry Potter films, Gambon was knighted by Queen Elizabeth II for services to drama in 1998.

The Beast Must Die concerns wealthy playboy, philanthropist and big game hunter Tom Newcliffe (Calvin Lockhart). Newcliffe invites, as you do, an eclectic group of people to his gigantic country mansion as guests of him and his wife Caroline (Marlene Clark) because he is convinced that one of these characters is a werewolf! The sprawling mansion is fitted with a high-tech closed-circuit television surveillance system with numerous security cameras and listening devices controlled by Newcliffe's trusted assistant and employee Pavel (Anton Diffring). Once the werewolf is secretly spied or duly reveals his or her self, Newcliffe plans to shoot the biggest game of all with his hunting rifle and add it to his prized trophy collection.

This select group of suspects is made up of archaeology and werewolf expert Dr Lundgren (Peter Cushing), former medical student and suspected cannibal Paul Foote (Tom Chadbon), disgraced British diplomat with constantly disappearing staff Arthur Bennington (Charles Gray), society beauty Davinia Gilmore (Ciaran Madden), and shifty looking concert pianist Jan Jarmokowski (Michael Gambon), a man who (suspiciously) never seems too geographically far away from the scene of some grisly murder. "Why do you think I invited you? Because every one of you sitting right here in this room has one thing in common: Death!" declares Newcliffe. He's completely obsessed with bagging a werewolf and dismisses the servants and cuts off the telephones. He insists that his guests all stay throughout the cycle of the full moon until the beast reveals itself.

As our suspects play chess, banter, dine and discuss werewolf lore at Newcliffe's grand country house, numerous red herrings and clues are thrown in our direction and the film even invites us to guess who we think the werewolf might be, supplying us with an enjoyably gimmicky William Castle style thirty second 'Werewolf Break' (narrated by Valentine Dyall) with ticking clock before the great revelation. The Beast Must Die begins by telling us that "This is a detective story in which YOU are the detective. The question is not WHO is the murderer? - But WHO is the werewolf? After all the clues have been shown YOU will get a chance to give your answer. Watch for the werewolf break!"

The Beast Must Die is sort of Agatha Christie meets Shaft (leading man Calvin Lockhart comes across a more theatrical Shaft clone) meets The Most Dangerous Game meets James Bond meets a low-budget Amicus film. Newcliffe seems to have a fondness for James Bond style gadgetry and the introduction to his character is very Bondish. It begins with some wonderfully funky and amusing seventies music courtesy of the always dependable Douglas Gamley and sweeping overhead shots of isolated countryside. Calvin Lockhart, wearing the first in a succession of slightly camp tight outfits that frequently make him look like a backing singer in the Eurovision song contest, is being hunted in a booby trapped forest by numerous armed men.

He eventually crashes exhausted through the foliage onto genteel lawns by his mansion where his guests/werewolf suspects are politely sipping tea outside and waiting for him. The armed men of course were all Newcliffe employees and he was merely testing his security system using himself as bait! The guests must know why they are really here and quickly start to bicker and look shifty when Newcliffe drops his - on the face of it completely bonkers - werewolf bombshell. "You're not seriously trying to tell us that one of us is a Werewolf!" protests Michael Gambon, looking a bit like Jason King. It's quite a nice idea to try and cross a drawing room murder mystery with a werewolf film and The Beast Must Die always keeps you interested to find out who the culprit is, especially when the murders begin.

The clues and red herrings are a bit all over the place to say the least and not to be taken too seriously. This is really a film where they could probably have revealed anyone as the werewolf at the end after endowing virtually every single character in the whole film with at least one suspicious piece of behaviour or background information!

The film makes quite good use of the surrounding woods (the famous Amicus stream makes an appearance), overhead helicopter shots and the whole surveillance angle. Pavel's security room with countless television monitors watching over the mansion is nicely designed and enjoyable in a dated seventies sort of way with its chessboard floor and Pavel's electronic "grid" with little red lights indicating where his various listening devices are. The scenes between Diffring and Lockhart in the security room as they plot a way to flush out the werewolf are always good fun.

There is a car chase too involving Gambon that is slightly comical but enjoyable with Gamley's very seventies music pounding away. Perhaps one criticism is that the film is never very scary or frightening, instead often coming across as camp, but it is quite creepy on one or two occasions and there is a bit of blood and gore (though not much) here and there when the guests start to be picked off. One of the most atmospheric and memorable scenes in the film probably occurs when Pavel's security room is threatened by the werewolf from a glass ceiling high above.

The werewolf itself, when it finally makes an appearance, is quite obviously a large German Shepard dog with a big coat thrown over it or something and as you are always patently aware of this fact they wisely don't overdo the werewolf capers. At least you get a vague sense of a live beast on the loose even if it isn't terribly convincing or terrifying. The alternative of an actor pitching up with a Dog Soldiers type werewolf mask probably wouldn't have improved the film an awful lot in my opinion. The werewolf shenanigans work best when they are depicted in a relatively fleeting manner or occur during the quite atmospheric sequences which are set during the night.

Today they would CG a film like The Beast Must Die to within an inch of its life and probably lose half of the charm on offer here. The central idea of the film, that one of the guests is really a werewolf but must hide that fact, is always more interesting and creepy than the actual 'werewolf' scenes that occur. The Beast Must Die has a rather eccentric cast and it's always enjoyable to see them together at the dinner table with vast tracts of werewolf information and musings on things like transmogrification entertainingly coming from Peter Cushing's Dr Lundgren courtesy of a bizarre foreign accent. "Ze urge to eat human flesh iz uncontrollable," explains Lundgren as they sit around the dinner table. "I'm afraid der iz vorse to come..." I don't know about anyone else but he'd certainly put me off my Crispy Pancakes and potato waffles if he came around for tea.

Cushing nonetheless engages and gains sympathy in his usual quiet way and Michael Gambon and Tom Chadbon are both fun just for their ridiculous seventies hair and clothes. The frilly shirts and period trappings form part of the charm of the film now. The urbane Charles Gray is sadly a trifle underused though as Arthur Bennington and mostly just complains about being held against his will by Newcliffe. I think I would have liked a bit more for Anton Diffring to do as Newcliffe's right hand man Pavel too. Diffring spends most of the film in the high-tech surveillance attempting to track the werewolf for his boss. He's also supposed to be from the country where the werewolves originated so is yet another suspect in the film!

The scenes of these characters all together in the mansion are always good fun though and I love the moment when the guests are presented with a blood red sauce at dinner, presumably to entice the werewolf into a slip. "Well, if that was dinner, I can't wait for the cabaret!" says Rick Wakeman lookalike Tom Chadbon. Newcliffe deploys various (and not very subtle) methods in the film designed to make one of his guests suddenly sprout fur and grow fangs so there is plenty of riffing on werewolf mythology with the passing around of silver candlesticks and bullets etc. "Money buys things but men shape events!" says Newcliffe, attempting to explain his obsession to nab a pesky werewolf.

A big part of the cult appeal of The Beast Must Die is surely the eccentric and strange performance of Calvin Lockhart as Newcliffe. Lockhart is ridiculously hammy and theatrical and has a habit of suddenly emphasising random words as if he's trying desperately to impart great weight and meaning. It is a slightly odd spectacle at times with this over enunciating Shaft clone attempting to prod a collection of refined actors into tripping up and turning into a werewolf. Lockhart's earnestly wooden performance and choice range of camp outfits is a winning combination and it's always oddly compelling when he's running around in the woods with his hunting rifle and an outfit that wouldn't look out of place in an episode of Blake's 7.

Despite my affectionate jesting of Lockhart's thesping prowess I do genuinely enjoy his performance in the film and he's always a commanding and rather stylish presence in his black, slightly military style outfits as the guests mince about in a selection of lighter summer clobber and silly hats. Despite its obvious flaws and rather modest budget, The Beast Must Die is hugely enjoyable nonsense on the whole with a great central premise (I'm amazed to be honest that no one has ever thought of remaking this). This is an entertaining dose of kitsch seventies British horror with a host of familiar faces. And no, the first time I watched this I didn't manage to guess correctly who the werewolf was! Watch out for the "werewolf break" and see if you have better luck than I did.

THE LAND THAT TIME FORGOT (1974)

The Land That Time Forgot was directed by Kevin Connor and written by Michael Moorcock and James Cawthorn. It is based on the 1924 novel of the same name by Edgar Rice Burroughs. This film was a co-production with AIP and with a budget of a million pounds was the most expensive film Amicus had made. We've reached the final phase in the Amicus story. The ahistorical family friendly adventure capers with Doug McClure, dinosaurs, and monsters galore. Those of a certain age will have fond memories of watching The Land That Time Forgot a gazillion times on television growing up.

"To be honest, I sort of fell into the Edgar Rice Burroughs

world thanks to Milton Subotsky and Max Rosenberg at Amicus," said the director Kevin Connor. "They liked what I did with Beyond the Grave and offered me Land That Time Forgot and it went from there for several years. Just a great time and fun making those monsters on such low budgets. It was a good script and I was surrounded by great technicians like Alan Hume (DP) and Maurice Carter (Production Designer). All the monsters were hand puppets designed by Roger Dickens. We shot the opening sequence up in Skye – buzzing about in a helicopter. Wonderful memories of an innocent time."

Kevin Connor began what would become a frequent partnership with Doug McClure on this film. You could say that Doug McClure was Kurt Russell to Kevin Connor's John Carpenter! Well, maybe not but you get my point. Kevin Connor's career fizzled out in the end into Hallmark Christmas films but he did direct the cultish horror film Motel Hell. Stuart Whitman was initially chosen by Amicus to be the lead in The Land That Time Forgot but AIP (for reasons best known to themselves) refused to finance the film with Whitman - which opened the door for Doug McClure. McClure was a film and television veteran. He made a lot of television films in the 1970s so being the lead in The Land That Time Forgot was quite nice you'd imagine.

John McEnery, who plays Captain Von Schoenvorts in the film, was married to Stephanie Beacham at the time. McEnery was dubbed by Anton Diffring in the film because the producers were not too convinced by the German accent that McEnery did. The reliable Keith Baron, who plays Bradley in this film, would go on to be a familiar face to British viewers on television by appearing in literally everything. He was probably best known for that terrible sitcom Duty Free - where the characters are supposed to be in Spain but it was all shot at a television studio in Leeds!

Susan Penhaligon had a very interesting career in the 1970s. Penhaligon was in Pete Walker's House of Mortal Sin and Paul Verhoeven's Soldier of Orange. She was also in the cultish Ozploitation film Patrick. She was dubbed the British Bardot at one point but her career fizzled out somewhat in the 1980s and she did more television and stage work later on rather than films. Anthony Ainley, who plays Dietz in The Land That Time Forgot, would become best known for his role as the Master in Doctor Who.

The story begins with narration by a weary narrator, his message in a bottle picked up by a sailor. "I do not expect anyone to believe the story that I am about to relate. It even seems incredible to me that all that I have passed through, all those weird and terrifying experiences, should have been encompassed within as short a span as three brief months. It must have been a little after 3 o'clock in the afternoon that it began - the afternoon of June 3rd, 1916."

The narrator is an American named Bowen Tyler (Doug McClure). You might say that Bowen has had quite an experience. He survived a German U-boat attack on a passenger ship and - along with Lisa Clayton (Susan Penhaligon) - was picked up by British sailors who survived too. Bowen reasoned that their only chance of survival was to wrest control of the U-boat when it surfaced and so a battle commenced and they were successful. However, their search for a British port is scuppered by a lack of fuel. They end up near the South Pole where they discover Caprona - a lost world of dinosaurs and neanderthals! The Germans and the sailors must now work together as they dodge dinosaurs and numerous hazards in this mysterious lost landmass.

The Land That Time Forgot is a likeable B-movie with real heart. It is impossible not to have at least some affection for this trilogy of adventure films Amicus made at the end of their wonderfully entertaining contribution to British cinema. Anything goes in these films. Doug McClure battling monsters that look like oversized rubber chickens, subterranean caves, lost civilisations, dinosaurs. These films were successful too. In 1978, Doug McClure and Kevin Connor even made Warlords of Atlantis together for EMI to quench the thirst of those happy to see more of these types of films. Amicus had sadly wound up by then but Warlords of Atlantis is like another Amicus film in all but name.

Take B-movies today, or what passes for them. The all too knowing Sharknadoesque films with their comedy guest stars and soulless CGI. The Land That Time Forgot isn't winking at the camera or desperately trying to be tongue-in-cheek or stupid. It's just trying to give you a good time and do the best job that it can with the budget available. Yes, The Land That Time Forgot is a silly film at times but it's a silly film with a lot of charm and some wonderful old fashioned special effects. The miniatures and models of ships, submarines and ice glazed caves are all very good.

"Some of the effects are bit 'cringe worthy' when you see them today," said Kevin Connor in an interview years later. "But you have to take them in the time they were created – and the low budget, of course – so I don't feel too bad about it. The submarine stuff was excellent I thought and still stands up today. I was very involved with all aspects of the production. The reason we went for the hand puppets was for a more fluid look. Roger Dicken, who created the dinosaurs did such fine details and had the movement down so well that we went with him and used that technique. Also, we developed the use of a small VistaVision camera to shoot the dinosaur back-ground plates which gave us great quality because the exposed frame is twice the size of a normal 35mm. Everything was shot front projection as well."

Naturally, the dinosaurs in The Land That Time Forgot are not exactly state of the art (I gather that Amicus decided against stop-motion effects for the monsters because they felt this would be too time consuming and costly) but they are fun. If you did want to be nitpicky you'd probably say that some of the back projection work is poor. Back projection was a blight of many films in this era. It just never looked convincing. The cast in The Land That Time Forgot is pretty solid for a film of this type. Anthony Ainley as the shadowy Dietz and John McEnery as Captain Von Schoenvorts in particular. It's a nice touch by the way that the Germans agree to work together with Doug McClure and company when the dinosaur doo doo hits the fan. Who cares about World War I anymore when you are lost in Caprona?

Doug McClure is often remembered as a naff B-film actor but this broad brush is a trifle unfair. McClure is actually a solid leading man here for the film to anchor itself around. He was terrific around this time in a great television film called Satan's Triangle and had been acting long enough to be in legendary shows like The Twilight Zone. McClure was sort of like William Shatner or Roger Moore. One of those actors who people lampooned but who was better than they were ever given any credit for. You've got good support too from the ever reliable Keith Barron and Susan Penhaligon is the damsel and female lead.

The Land That Time Forgot is rather like a low budget British version of Jurassic Park made decades before the Spielberg film. The puppet dinosaurs are unavoidably hokey at times but they have personality and the atmosphere of this lush creature festooned secret world is always well conveyed with plenty of danger abounding for our heroes. This film is very competently directed by Connor and remains a lot of fun for adventure and dinosaur fans of all ages. It's interesting the way that Amicus had come full circle in their last years. They started off with musical films and the Dr Who adventures. Here they are now, nearly at the end, back to making family films. The Land That Time Forgot was profitable and so therefore guaranteed that Amicus would continue down this path of family adventure films - which is a slight shame because who wouldn't have loved another Amicus horror film? From a strictly business point of view though you couldn't argue with the logic.

AT THE EARTH'S CORE (1976)

At the Earth's Core was directed by Kevin Connor and based on the fantasy novel of the same name by Edgar Rice Burroughs. Milton Subotsky was responsible for the screenplay. This is more child friendly monster mayhem from Amicus. Doug McClure returned as the lead again and Peter Cushing also returned to Amicus to star alongside him. As if that wasn't enough you also get Caroline Munro as Princess Dia. In the 1970s, Munro transitioned from modelling to acting and gained recognition for her roles in Hammer horror films, such as Dracula A.D. 1972 and Captain Kronos – Vampire Hunter. She also appeared in Dr Phibes Rises Again and the James Bond film The Spy Who Loved Me. Caroline Munro continued to work in the horror and science fiction genres throughout the 1980s and 1990s, appearing in films such as Maniac, The Last Horror Film, and Slaughter High.

I for one hold a bizarre fondness for Starcrash - which is surely one of Caroline's most memorable roles. Starcrash is a famously bad 1979 Italian Star Wars clone directed by Luigi Cozzi, a Spaghetti Star Wars if you will. The film has though become a minor kitsch cult classic in the years since its release, primarily for the presence of Caroline Munro in some scandalously flesh revealing costumes but also because it is just a very surreal and very amusing experience. Starcrash haphazardly blends together the aforementioned 1977 George Lucas space opera, Barbarella, and Jason and the Argonauts (amongst others) with a jaw-dropping ineptness not witnessed since the days of Ed Wood. The air of cluelessness that pervades the story and production of Starcrash is only equalled by the bonkers cast, none of whom appear to even be in the same film let alone on the same page.

Cy Grant, who plays Ra in At the Earth's Core, was a Guyanese stage actor who served in the RAF during the war. Cy was one of the first black people to feature on British television. He was also the voice of Lieutenant Green in Gerry Anderson's Captain Scarlet and the Mysterons. Anyway, what is the premise of At the Earth's Core? I'm glad you asked. David Innes (Doug McClure) has financed a remarkable scientific project. A huge drilling vehicle (that looks like something out of Thunderbirds) known as the Iron Mole. The brains behind this Victorian steampunk marvel is Dr Abner Perry (Peter Cushing), an inventor and scientist.

The duo decide to test out the Iron Mole on a Welsh mountain (I'm sure the local tourist board were thrilled about this!) but get far more than they bargained for when they drill into the Earth's core and end up in a land called Pellucidar. Those Nazi theories about a Hollow Earth must have been right after all. In the centre of the Earth is a strange prehistoric world full of strange dinosaurs and cavemen who look like hippies. It is ruled by the evil Mahars, a race that enslave through mind control. Will our plucky heroes manage to survive this most outlandish of Hollow Earth capers?

At the Earth's Core feels more cartoony and constrictive than The Land That Time Forgot but as long as you aren't expecting Raiders of the Lost Ark then there is fun to be had here. One would say though that this is arguably the weakest of the three adventure films that Kevin Connor made for the studio. Pellucidar is quite stage bound (as opposed to the location work we got in The Land That Time Forgot and The People That Time Forgot) but enjoyably surreal all the same with a vivid pink hue washing over the caves and plastic shrubbery. The dinosaurs and monsters are all fascinatingly weird and seem like a melange of real creatures and mythical beasts. The special effects are very much of the old Japanese Godzilla film variety. Actors are dressed up in monster suits and grapple away, superimposed into the backdrop as the actors look on in alarm.

This is unavoidably a very silly film and some of the monsters and special effects are laughable but then I don't think anyone is supposed to be taking this seriously or subjecting it to immense critical scrutiny. "Basically my movies for Amicus were Saturday morning movies – except of course for Beyond The Grave!" said Kevin Connor. "They had no pretensions and I always liked to think that the audiences enjoyed watching them as much as I enjoyed making them. I'd like to think that the big special FX movies that followed were even minutely influenced by me – but I suspect not. Our FX were so crude by comparison to the standards set by George Lucas and Steven Spielberg. They had bigger budgets and the technology had leapt forward. I wish we had followed that path but Amicus folded in the late 70's – sadly. It was a great place for first time directors to start."

At the Earth's Core is just a colourful Saturday morning kids adventure film made on a modest budget - although the one and half million pounds they apparently spent on this caper was more money than Amicus had ever spent before. To put it into context, look at the big films of 1976. The James Bond film The Spy Who Loved Me cost fourteen million pounds to make. Shout at the Devil, a period adventure film starring Roger Moore, had a budget of ten million pounds. Jaws, which came out the previous year and features ONE solitary 'monster', cost nearly ten million pounds. Amicus were essentially trying to make a special effects laden monster adventure film on a relative shoestring.

The models are fun though in At the Earth's Core. The Iron Mole definitely looks like something out of a Gerry Anderson show and the control room is an enjoyably anachronistic Victorian creation with plush wood panels and what look like television screens. It's fun when Dr Perry and David are thrown around as this machine burrows into the ground and the control room is shaken up. It's very Victorian the way that Perry whacks the controls with an umbrella whenever they start to malfunction or become obstreperous!

Peter Cushing joins the mayhem in At the Earth's Core and deploys the 'doddery old man' character that he used in the Dr Who films - only even more doddery and comic. This is hardly the finest hour of Peter Cushing but he's good fun in the film as this crackpot Victorian inventor. I like the sight of Cushing in a top hat at the start of the film. Doug McClure gets to sport a preposterous striped blazer too at the beginning of the film. The costume department certainly had a sense of humour.

The best thing about the film is the addition of Hammer 'babe' Caroline Munro as Princess Dia, the slavegirl love interest for McClure. Munro livens up any film from this era and always makes the cast of anything much more cultish. It's a shame though that Munro disappears for a chunk of the story. They should definitely have beefed her part up a lot more. If you've got Caroline Munro in your cast it's a crime not to use her as much as possible. At the Earth's Core is daft fun for the undemanding younger viewers and those with a soft spot for silly creature features. It feels like a step down somewhat from The Land That Time Forgot but if you park your brain in neutral there is some fun on offer here in one of the silliest films ever produced by the wonderful Amicus studio.

At the Earth's Core was again fairly profitable - though the higher than usual budget for Amicus must have cut into the profits a bit. This is a very daft film but it is very charming too with its old school special effects and lack of pretension. At the Earth's Core was not a film made for critics to nitpick or laugh at. It is not a film where we are supposed to pick apart the plot and acting. It was made to entertain kids on a Saturday morning. Oh, and the joke at the end of the film is actually quite clever and funny.

THE PEOPLE THAT TIME FORGOT (1977)

The People That Time Forgot was the last film made by Amicus Productions. They actually dissolved before the film was released - which meant AIP got the credit. Max Rosenberg has the sole producer credit because Milton Subotsky had left Amicus. Rosenberg kept the show on the road for a few years alone and then the company was wound up. Times were changing fast in the dystopian rubble strewn future year of 1977. A time of economic crisis, moral panic, Roger Moore playing James Bond in a pair of cream flares, and a very special birthday for the Queen. A bunch of scruffy herberts known as The Sex Pistols had become public enemy number one but they have the last laugh on their critics by producing one of the most greatest British albums of all time.

For the twilight film of Amicus, Kevin Connor returned to direct The People That Time Forgot and Patrick Tilley's script was based on The People That Time Forgot (1924) and Out of Time's Abyss (1924) by Edgar Rice Burroughs. The film is a direct sequel to The Land That Time Forget. Doug McClure is back but only in an extended cameo though as Patrick Wayne is the lead. Patrick Wayne is the son of John Wayne. Patrick made a lot of films and appeared in many television shows but he never became a star. That could have changed though. He was offered the role of Superman in the 1978 film but dropped out when his father fell ill. This opened the door for a young unknown actor called Christopher Reeve to take the role.

The People That Time Forgot was an early film role for Sarah Douglas. She'd done some bits and pieces on television - including Space 1999. She would shortly get her most famous role - that of Kryptonian supervillain Ursa in Superman and Superman II. There are a smattering of familiar faces in the rest of the cast. Vintage heavy Milton Reid (he was the little burly chap that James Bond fought on a roof in Egypt in The Spy Who Loved Me) as one of a race of warriors and Tony Britton as the captain of the naval ship. You'll also spy David Prowse in this film too. Sadly, there is no Susan Penhaligon. She was obviously busy or too expensive to hire when this film was made as Bowen tells us that her character was sacrificed to a volcano!

Shane Rimmer, who plays Hogan in The People That Time Forgot, was a Canadian actor who spent his career in Britain. Shane was in Bond films, worked on Gerry Anderson's television shows, and was in everything from Tales of the Unexpected to Batman Begins. Dana Gillespie, who plays the cavegirl Ajor in The People That Time Forgot, is primarily a singer who has recorded dozens of albums. Dana was in Jesus Christ Superstar with Paul Nicholas in the early seventies. Dana and Paul actually made cameos in the 1972 Christmas episode of Till Death Us Do Part - where Alf Garnett runs into the cast of Jesus Christ Superstar in a boozer! Dana was in the Hammer film The Lost Continent and later appeared in the Nicholas Roeg film Bad Timing and the British borstal drama Scrubbers.

The plot in The People That Time has Major Ben McBride (Patrick Wayne) mounting an expedition to locate his old friend Bowen Tyler (Doug McClure), who, lest we forget, is stranded in Caprona. Once they reached the lost landmass by ship, McBride sets out in a biplane with the paleontologist Norfolk (Thorley Walters), mechanic Hogan (Shane Rimmer), and photographer Lady Charlotte 'Charly' Cunningham (Sarah Douglas). They are attacked by a pterodactyl (I hate it when that happens!) and end up trekking it on foot. Will they manage to find the elusive and stranded Tyler Bowen?

This last hurrah for Amicus is decent enough family fare although probably not as much cartoonish fun as the two films that came before. It feels slightly less silly if anything - which is either a good thing or a bad thing depending on one's perspective. Naturally, The People That Time Forgot is not a Ken Loach film but it is more conventional and less campy than something like At the Earth's Core. The People That Time Forgot reminds me somewhat of those cheapjack Allan Quatermain films that Cannon made with Richard Chamberlain in the eighties. Patrick Wayne is something of a humourless block of wood in the lead role and always feels like he is reading his lines off cue cards but Sarah Douglas is quite charismatic and playful as the female lead Charly. Douglas has a Princess Leia hairstyle and seems to be enjoying herself.

The veteran Thorley Walters and the ever reliable Shane Rimmer (famous for roles in gazillions of British films and television shows) are both very good as supporting characters too. By surrounding Patrick Wayne with this gang they manage to mitigate somewhat the lack of charisma and zero acting range evident in the leading man. The People That Time Forgot seems to have a smaller budget than the previous two Amicus adventure films and there aren't as many monsters and dinosaurs or as many outrageously campy sets. This feels like a restrained production at times compared to the previous two Amicus family films it follows but I suppose it's possible too that Kevin Connor wanted to make this a slightly more conventional film.

As you'd expect, considering it is a sequel, The People That Time Forgot is much more of a blood relative to The Land That Time Forgot than it is to At the Earth's Core.

Much of The People That Time Forgot is shot on location (in Spain) outdoors and the characters never really feel as if they are on a lost continent. They could literally be anywhere with a few rocks and some hills. I suppose one could argue though the real location work gives it more of an authentic 'movie' feel and there are some nice panorama shots of the characters trekking through the hills and mountains.

The special effects in The People That Time Forgot are a bit on the dodgy side (the back projection for the biplane scenes in particular is very dated and unconvincing) but the quirky Douglas, Walters, and the always dependable Shane Rimmer help to keep the film afloat. The supporting cast around Wayne do steer the film through a few lulls and some of the more obvious flaws in the story and the production. Disappointingly, Doug McClure only has a glorified cameo in this. He's like Charlton Heston in Beneath the Planet of the Apes! They only find him near the end so he doesn't feature much.

The People That Time Forgot does get a bit more fun during the subterranean section near the end - which provides some welcome weirdness and camp and is a respite from scenes of the characters walking up rocky hills with rubber dinosaurs occasionally popping up. The People That Time Forgot is a passable time filler although a little low-key compared to the more outrageous pulp and sci-fi on offer in The Land That Time Forgot and At the Earth's Core. It could have been better but it's by no means a terrible film and those who have a fondness for old school special effects and B-movies from yesteryear will certainly find something to enjoy.

Sadly, this film marked the end of the Amicus story. It's a shame indeed that they couldn't have stuck around to build on the foundations of these adventure films (which were quite popular at the time) and even perhaps delve back into horror. What an amazingly fun legacy Amicus left behind though. The People That Time Forgot turned a tidy profit but Amicus were no longer around to enjoy that success. So what happened to Milton Subotsky and Max Rosenberg next? Well, let's find out in our concluding section.

AFTERMATH

Before we go forward we should go back for a brief interlude and mention 1960's The City of the Dead. The City of the Dead was directed by John Llewellyn Moxey and written by George Baxt. This isn't an official Amicus film but it might as well be. It was produced by Max Rosenberg and Milton Subotsky under their production company Vulcan (this was the only film made under that banner). A few years later they took the name

Amicus and the rest is history. So, with this in mind, any book about about Amicus that didn't mention The City of the Dead would feel incomplete. The City of the Dead is really more or less an Amicus film. More than that though, The City of the Dead is a brilliant little horror film that deserves to be much better known. If this film was made by Hammer it would be a cult classic.

The City of the Dead was made in Britain (at Shepperton) but is set in the United States. Which would explain why Christopher Lee is grappling with an American accent! The script started life as a pilot for a proposed Boris Karloff television series but this show obviously didn't transpire in the end. The City of the Dead was released in the United States in 1961 under the (rather silly) title Horror Hotel. The American version of The City of the Dead suffered some cuts by the censors and was missing some key scenes.

The story begins in 1692. A witch named Elizabeth Selwyn is burned at the stake but summons supernatural powers to save herself. "In 1692, Elizabeth Selwyn went to the stake, she was buried in the churchyard in New England, and yet 3 years later, 3 years later a new wave of blood sacrifices broke out in the village that condemned her. The daughters of the elders who had condemned her were themselves found dead with every single drop of blood drained from their bodies, and afterwards people came forward to testify that they had actually seen Elizabeth Selwyn." This is a great sequence and very vivid and horrific. The City of the Dead often manages to convey a feverish dream/nightmare atmosphere where we can't always be sure what is real or not. Despite the fact that it was made in 1959, The City of the Dead uses many techniques that feel very modern. You get 'jump scares' and a nice amping up of tension at times.

After the prologue, we go back to the present day where Nan Barlow (Venetia Stevenson) is a curious and attentive student who studies witchcraft in the classes of Professor Alan Driscoll (Christopher Lee). I don't remember A'Level witchcraft at school! I would definitely have taken that class. Nan is persuaded by Driscoll to visit a Massachusetts town called Whitewood that has a long and dark history when it comes to witchcraft and alleged witches. Nan is told that she can learn a lot more about the history of witchcraft in Whitewood and gain some valuable knowledge to prepare herself for her exams. So, Nan travels to this out of the way little town and settles into the Raven's Inn. However, the eccentric owner Mrs Newless (Patricia Jessel) and the locals seem more than a little strange. There is something very weird about this town - as Nan will discover for herself.

The City of the Dead is a beautiful looking horror film with the black and white photography and smoke billowed anachronistic village. This film really does look amazing at times. It's like an episode of The Twilight Zone crossed with Night of the Living Dead. As Nan gets closer and closer to Whitead, the landscape becomes ever more nightmarish and mist shrouded. We begin to develop an unease. No good can come of this visit to Whitewood, we strongly suspect. Maybe it's because it was made around the same time as the first season of Rod Serling's Twilight Zone and also uses black and white and modest studio sets, but The City of the Dead really does feel like watching an elongated 'lost' Twilight Zone episode at times.

It's hard to go into depth with the plot without giving everything away but it is remarkable all the same how much this film is like Psycho (which was released a few months before The City of the Dead but actually went production a month LATER than this film). Both films have an identical structure in the way that they make you think a certain person is the main character and then completely flip that assumption on its head in shocking fashion. Both films then have similar second and third acts with family/friends investigating a disappearance and they even have a similar shocking 'rocking chair' reveal. It's incredible how these two films seem to be so similar in their structure.

This is arguably the scariest film that Rosenberg and Subotsky ever made and has some genuinely tense and creepy moments of horror. You genuinely fear for the characters in The City of the Dead. You should beware of the shorter American cut of this film that is still floating around. That version omits the witch burning scene at the start, presumably because it was deemed too shocking for the censors at the time. This scene is not only very arresting though but seagues into the class being taught by Professor Driscoll. It's a very fun theatrical sequence of horror and feels like it should always be a part of the film.

Christopher Lee's American accent is passable enough (even if he doesn't seem entirely comfortable with it) and his performance is commanding enough too for the part. The director has some striking close ups of Lee looking stern and sinister in the film. Venetia Stevenson, who retired from acting not long after The City of the Dead, is likeable enough as the young student. Her performance in this film isn't widely appreciated (it seems - from retrospective reviews) but I like her slightly mannered accent and down to earth nature. Patricia Jessel adds some flamboyance to the cast and Dennis Lotis and Tom Naylor are serviceable enough when they take on more of a central role in the story.

One might argue though that the first half of The City of the Dead is stronger as we learn more about the town through the window of Venetia Stevenson's character. Like her, we get drips and drabs of information and begin to suspect that something is very wrong about this place. The mythology of the story in the film is the sort of thing that The Blair Witch Project traded on. There are some very effective scenes in the film where Nan seems to hear voices and music and evidence of a party but is only met with an empty quiet room when she investigates or tries to join the fun. These scenes are very effective in conveying the strange nature of Whitehood, a place where reality and nightmares seem to be merging into one.

The City of the Dead is a great looking and effective horror film that is still very enjoyable. Rarely have fog machines and low budget sets been made to look so striking and chilling. This is an important film in the Amicus story too because it obviously gave Rosenberg and Subotsky experience and confidence when it came to producing horror films. It was a genre they would memorably return to three years under the Amicus name.

Amicus dissolved around the time they made The People That Time Forgot and Subotsky and Rosenberg went their separate ways - although both continued to work in the film industry. Both Hammer and Amicus bit the dust in the seventies but Hammer did make an attempt to forge a new life on television with Hammer House of Horror and Hammer House of Mystery & Suspense in the 1980s. Milton Subotsky had plans at one point to make an Amicus television show in the horror anthology vein but sadly this never transpired. One of the contributing factors (besides finance issues obviously) in the demise of the British horror film industry was the influx of a new wave of American horror films like Night of the Living Dead, The Texas Chainsaw Massacre and The Exorcist.

The Amicus films suddenly looked very twee and old-fashioned when contrasted against something like The Exorcist. Times were changing. With the passage of time though the Amicus anthology films in particular have been rediscovered by new generations who love them for their seventies period trappings and Britishness. Milton Subotsky was sometimes criticised for making the anthology pictures too tame (he didn't like nudity and violence) but perhaps that might be part of the charm now? There was never anything too distasteful about the films. They were also morality tales in the EC tradition so likeable for this reason.

Milton Subotsky's wife Fiona said many years later in an interview that although she didn't know what the precise details were of the falling out between Milton and Max Rosenberg she had a fairly good idea. They likely fell out over money and control of Amicus. This led to legal battles between them. Milton seemed to lose interest in Amicus in the middle of their final phase of family adventure films. It could be the case that Milton felt these types of films were not his cup of tea and yearned to go back to horror. Subotsky was clearly a fan of the anthology format because some of his post-Amicus credits were also horror compendium films. In the wake of the demise of Amicus, Subotsky formed his own production company (Sword & Sorcery Productions) and had many plans (including films based on Conan and The Incredible Hulk) but few came to fruition.

Why was this? Perhaps it was because Max Rosenberg was the money man with the head for business while Milton was more of an ideas man (I should add though that Max Rosenberg denied this common summation of their partnership and always insisted he was very 'hands-on' in the making of the films). Milton Subotsky's wife Fiona said that when Amicus dissolved and Milton started up on his own again it was more difficult to finance films in Britain than it had been in the 1960s and early 1970s. This was presumably why Milton - though by a British citizen by now - drifted back to the United States to make some films.

Subotsky was back on familiar ground in 1977 for The Uncanny. He was the co-producer of this Rank Organisation distributed film. The Uncanny is a British/Canadian horror anthology film directed by Denis Héroux. This is probably second only to Tales That Witness Madness for sheer ludicrousness when it comes to seventies horror anthologies. The Uncanny offers three tales of horror all revolving around cats and opens in Montreal where nervous author Wilbur Gray (the great Peter Cushing) goes to visit his publisher Frank Richards (Ray Milland) with his latest book - all the while being secretly followed by a black moggy. Gray has written about flying saucers and the secrets of the pyramids in the past but his latest offering looks set to be his most eccentric work yet.

The dubious publisher listens as Gray explains that he has discovered that cats secretly run the world and his book will prove it. "You let them prowl about just as they please, hardly noticing them, and all the time they're watching us, spying on us, making sure we behave. Cats have been exploiting the human race for centuries!" Richards, despite the presence of his own cat making Gray even more nervous, is not entirely convinced by what appears to be a completely barmy suggestion but listens while the author presents three strange cases in an attempt to prove his theory.

The first story is set in London in 1912. Wealthy bedridden dowager Miss Malkin (Joan Greenwood) has a house full of cats and plans to leave them everything in her will to spite her selfish nephew Michael (Simon Williams). Her maid Janet (Susan Penhaligon) gets wind of this plan though when solicitor Wallace (Roland Culver) visits the house and leaves a copy of the will in his briefcase in the hall. During dinner later on in town, Janet tells Michael and shows him the copy of the will she secretly took. Unsurprisingly, Michael is a bit annoyed that his inheritance is going to a load of cats instead of him and tells Janet that she must get hold of the other will in Miss Malkin's safe so they can destroy it. Janet must accomplish this task without waking her cat loving employer but with the house full of the furry scamps this will be easier said than done.

There is no great twist in this story but it's certainly the strongest of the three tales in The Uncanny and the only one that feels very British. There are one or two macabre revelations and the sight of Susan Penhaligon fending off numerous cats is always quite amusing when it occurs. It's fairly obvious that an awful lot of editing and sound-effects have gone into vainly trying to make a bunch of tame, bored looking cats look like they are trying to claw Janet the maid to death. The story is not without intentional humour at times too - like a bit where Susan Penhaligon is trapped in a pantry with only cat food to eat!

The second story is set in Quebec Province in 1975. After the death of her parents in a plane crash, young Lucy (Katrina Holden Bronson) has to go and live with her only relative Mrs Blake (Alexandra Stewart). Mrs Blake is exactly not a barrel of laughs though and even worse is her stuck up bully of a daughter Angela (Chloe Franks) - who makes Lucy's life a misery with her remote controlled plane hijinks and general lack of sensitivity about Lucy being an orphan. Lucy's only solace comes in the form of her beloved cat Wellington and some memories of her mother, including some occult black magic books. Lucy is therefore not amused when Wellington is threatened with the boot because Angela keeps blaming him for accidents she caused.

This second segment, with its Canadian setting and dubbed voices, feels less effective and more generic than the first one. The Uncanny was a co-production between Rank and Montreal's Astral Films and it's a little jarring at times to go from the quintessentially British opening story into this. It does at least have a fun ending and Chloe Franks, who, as we have noted, was quite a busy child actor in this era, is suitably snotty as the irritating Angela - though Franks seems to be dubbed in the film. Generally though this second segment is fairly thin gruel for the horror anthology connoisseur.

The final story in The Uncanny is set in Hollywood in 1936. Thirties ham actor Valentine De'ath (Donald Pleasance) does away with his wife in inventive fashion through an on set accident and replaces her with his dim girlfriend Edina (Samantha Eggar) both onscreen and off. Problems only arise from his late wife's cat - who still lives at the house and duly enters into an escalating battle of wits with De'ath, who is not a cat lover at all. Will De'ath dispense with this pesky moggy or will the cat get revenge for the death of its former owner? This is a so-so final story for the anthology that descends into Donald Pleasance versus a cat with some comic pratfalls and mildly enjoyable film set hijinks (where the health and safety regulations certainly leave something to be desired) in the vein of the Jon Pertwee segment of The House That Dripped Blood. It builds to an effective if predictable ending and Pleasance is always quite good fun in anything he turns up in even if this is not one of his best roles.

The Uncanny is not nearly as much fun as the Amicus anthologies and - like Tales That Witness Madness - comes across as an inferior knock off of the compendiums like Dr Terror's House of Horrors and Tales from the Crypt that Amicus rattled out. The first segment works best as it is the only purely British component and therefore feels like it wouldn't be out of place in a real Amicus film. The framing device is not bad though and it's fun to watch Peter Cushing and Ray Milland together as the paranoid Gray tries to convince his publisher that cats are not to be trusted. The sheer absurdity of The Uncanny's central conceit is not without a bonkers charm. It's not up to Amicus standards but The Uncanny is just about worth a look for those with a completist weakness for seventies portmanteau horror films.

Milton Subotsky's new company Sword & Sorcery Productions were only responsible for two films in the end. The first was Dominique - a 1978 horror thriller directed by Michael Anderson. The film is based on the 1948 short story

What Beckoning Ghost by Harold Lawlor. Dominique stars Cliff Robertson as a businessman named David Ballard. Ballard lives in England with his rich wife Dominique (Jean Simmons). It is Dominique who has inherited wealth. She is the one keeps his business afloat and pays the gas bill in this family. Ballard has been playing mean tricks on Dominique though in order to make her go insane. He wants to get rid of his wife so he can get his greedy paws on her money.

Ballard makes Dominique think the house is haunted and employs various tricks to make her began to question her increasingly frazzled grip on sanity. The diabolical scheme works in the end. Dominique commits suicide by hanging herself in the conservatory and Ballard is happy because he now has her money. But not so fast. She then begins to apparently haunt him from the grave and now Ballard is the one who has his sanity under question.

Dominique is basically like watching a mildly interesting fifteen minute segment of Rod Serling's Night Gallery stretched out into a feature length film. There is an awful lot of padding in this picture. We get endless shots of Cliff Robertson looking thoughtful or walking up and down the stairs. This must have been one of the easiest jobs of Robertson's career. He barely speaks in much of the film! There weren't too many lines for him to learn on the plane. The casting of the usually terrific Robertson is rather wasted. He often looks as if he hasn't the faintest idea what he is even acting in.

There are a raft of scenes in Dominique which play out with hardly any dialogue in order to (presumably) stretch out the running length. This all gives the film a slow burn quality that does rather tend to test your patience in the end. The actual look and atmosphere of the film is not unlike watching an episode of Hammer House of Mystery & Suspense, an anthology show that made a stock in trade of these types of murder/revenge/madness sort of stories.

Most of the action in Dominique is confined to the big house of Ballard and it is shot to look as shadowy and mysterious as possible. So shadowy in fact you can't barely see what is going on half the time! Although the story is highly derivative (you can't help feeling as if you've seen this sort of 'revenge from beyond the grave' plot done millions of times in horror and thriller films and television shows), the direction is competent and there are a slew of familiar faces in the cast.

You get Simon Ward in a plum role as Ballard's streetwise young chauffeur, plus Ron Moody, Michael Jayston, Jenny Agutter, Judy Geeson, Leslie Dwyer (aka the miserable Punch and Judy man from Hi-de-Hi!), David Tomlinson (from Mary Poppins and Bedknobs & Broomsticks), and Jack Warner. They really managed to get a load of famous actors crammed into this film. Not all of them have a lot to do but there many familiar faces who are fun to spot. I reckon Milton probably did that old trick of hiring some of these people for a couple of days and then shooting as much as possible with them!

One obvious criticism of Dominique is that the twist is quite easy to predict. It's not that difficult from a very early stage in the film to work out what is really going on. It's a common problem with thrillers like this. It's hard to come up with a twist sometimes that no one saw coming. Despite some interesting flourishes, Dominique is weakened by the predictable ending and a story that doesn't really justify the 100 minute running time. Dominique has the sort of plot that Tales of the Unexpected would have had done and dusted in twenty-five minutes. If you like slow burn mysteries though you might get some enjoyment out of this - for the cast if nothing else.

Subotsky was also the producer on The Monster Club - a 1980 British anthology horror film directed by Roy Ward Baker and based on the works of author R Chetwynd-Hayes. This was the last of the Sword & Sorcery productions. The film is a last gasp attempt to get the British horror compendium film back on its feet, or at least give it a fond farewell of sorts. The framing device for the three stories in The Monster Club features Vincent Price and John Carradine in a rather camp and dated bright garish nightclub/disco where all the patrons are apparently monsters of some kind - although this conveyed by and large by Halloween masks for (presumably) budgetary reasons.

Price plays Count Erasmus, a kindly older vampire who, feeling a bit peckish, takes a nip of horror writer "R Chetwynd-

Hayes" (Carradine) while out and about at night. Erasmus is decent enough not to take too deep a bite though ("It's alright, you won't become one of us... ") and in order to show his gratitude for this welcome sup of blood he invites Chetwynd-Hayes, who he is happy to meet as one of his favourite authors, to the aforementioned club where all manner of strange things are loitering around including, most horrifically, a singer called B. A Robertson who (in addition to The Pretty Things) performs a few musical interludes with blue face make-up and fangs.

These music sections are so naff and embarrassing that you won't be able to get through repeat viewings of this film without use of the fast forward button on your remote control. I would dearly love an alternative cut of The Monster Club that got rid of B.A Robertson. But anyway, Chetwynd-Hayes, seeking inspiration for his stories, accepts the offer of a visit to "The Monster Club" and is shown a "monster genealogy chart" as Erasmus duly shares three spooky tales...

The first story (unlike the classic Amicus compendiums the separate segments are not individually titled here) on offer in The Monster Club revolves around scheming young couple George (Simon Ward) and Angela (Barbara Kellerman) who earn a living scamming and stealing from the rich. Things are not going well for this pair of hustling con artists though - until that is they spot a job advertisement in the paper asking for someone to work in a remote stately mansion cataloguing antiques.

Angela is persuaded to take the job by George, who is soon plotting to steal the fortune of the mysterious and deeply reclusive employer and owner of the mansion, a ghoulish and mysterious but gentle character known as Raven (James Laurenson). Angela, egged on by her heartless git of a boyfriend, pretends to be in love with Raven and the lonely bachelor eventually asks her to marry him - which makes it all the more tempting to string him along and find the right moment to pilfer the contents of his safe in the mansion. The only problem is that Raven is a monster hybrid known as a "Shadmock" and Shadmocks have a deadly secret power which they must always suppress for reasons that will become obvious over the course of this segment...

Despite the overt campiness and tongue-in-cheek nature of The Monster Club's disco framing device, the anthology does contain two mildly creepy stories with one or two chills and this first tale is one of them. The always watchable James Laurenson gives a strong and moving performance as the cursed Raven, doomed to a sad isolation in his huge mansion for fear of his secret ability - which has terrifying consequences if used - manifesting itself. He's a tragic figure, shuffling around his lonely manor grounds looking after his pigeons and falls hook, line and sinker for the pretty Angela's pretend affection.

This segment is always quite interesting and includes a really good sequence set at a lavish costumed ball full of people wearing masks which adds a nice element of weirdness and scope into the story. The single most memorable moment or twist in the film, and certainly the scariest, occurs in the final scene of this story which contains a good deal of tension towards the end. The final scene here is actually very EC Comics and more Creepshow than a camp compendium. Milton Subotsky said that The Monster Club was made for children but I'm not too sure the closing scene of this first segment is suitable for kids!

The second story in The Monster Club is more of a comic tale and is introduced by film producer "Lintom Busotsky" (obviously a pun on Milton Subotsky) as being based on his strange childhood. The young Lintom (Warren Saire) is bullied at school and curious to know why his father (Richard Johnson) only works at night and is never seen during the day. Even more strange is the clergyman (Donald Pleasence) who seems inordinately interested in the family. Warned by his mother (Britt Ekland) not to talk to strangers ("Beware of men with violin cases!" adds his father), young Lintom gradually comes to realise his family is not like other families and may soon be in danger...

Although it begins quite promisingly, this segment soon descends into farce and is therefore never that scary or intriguing ultimately. It comes as no surprise to learn that Lintom's father is a vampire and Pleasance and Anthony

Valentine are soon after him as inept vampire hunters. This is the weakest of the three segments here although Richard Johnson is quite good fun while Britt Ekland reminds us once again why she never quite managed to win that Oscar. I think there must be some sort of compendium horror curse on Britt because, like the Amicus anthology Asylum, she once again ends up in the weakest segment. It's nice of course to see Donald Pleasance too although this isn't one of his more memorable roles when it comes to his dabblings with British horror films.

The final story revolves around an American film director named Sam (Stuart Whitman) who is looking for the perfect spooky and authentic location while shooting a horror picture in Britain. "I'll find it myself at the weekend!" the frustrated Sam booms to his crew after not having much joy. The resulting drive takes him off the beaten track to a misty, primitive village that seems to belong to another time. Not only that but everybody there seems to be a ghoul of some sort with a fondness for digging up graves. The location is a bit too authentic for Sam who is soon eager to escape from this nutty place - with the help of friendly local ghoul Luna (Lesley Dunlop)...

This segment is a solid and atmospheric final addition to the anthology with an effective recurring nightmare feel and an enjoyable performance from Stuart Whitman who goes from arrogant and confident big shot film industry type to absolute scared desperation over the course of the story. The remote village location is nicely conveyed with copious use of the fog machine and the legendary and frequently barking mad Patrick Magee, veteran of Amicus compendium classics Asylum and Tales From the Crypt, also pops up in this story. He's actually quite subdued by his usual standards in The Monster Club!

The central premise here of someone becoming trapped in a strange isolated place and then being apparently unable to escape is always quite effective for horror purposes (I recall reading a Pan horror short story once that was similar to this segment) and is always quite well done in this tale with a suitably spooky twist ending. I think, out of the three stories in

The Monster Club, this is the one that you could imagine slotting quite nicely into any of the seventies Amicus compendiums. The climax to the first story is probably a trifle more horrifying than your typical Amicus fare and the second story is too lightweight and throwaway. This one though would have been a decent addition to things like Asylum and Vault of Horror.

The Monster Club doesn't have much of a reputation and seems to have been largely forgotten when it comes to British compendium horror films but is actually slightly better than you expect it to be with two decent segments. The nightclub scenes are - naturally - horribly dated but it is fun of course to see Vincent Price and John Carradine together, adding a touch of class to proceedings as they dispense various monster lore gibberish and even take to the dance floor at one point. Apparently, the Carradine role was intended for Christopher Lee but Lee was less than impressed with the title of the film and the prospect of sitting around in a spangly nightclub set and promptly turned it down!

The nightclub framing device does contain an inventive animated striptease down to the bone and - away from B. A Robertson and company - The Monster Club has a good score courtesy of John Georgiadis, Alan Hawkshaw and Amicus staple Douglas Gamley. The use of three composers gives each segment a different feel. The film suffers a little perhaps from its inconsistent tone and you'll either enjoy the naff musical interludes as a bit of camp dated fun or feel they affect the pacing of the film. I could have lived quite happily without them myself. While The Monster Club is not a classic, the presence of Price and Carradine and two reasonably decent and interesting segments make it worth a look for anyone interested in British compendium horror films.

Milton Subotsky worked in television next as the producer on 1981's The Martian Chronicles - which was partly made at Milton's old stomping ground Shepperton. The Martian Chronicles is a television science fiction miniseries based on the 1950 book of the same name by Ray Bradbury. It was directed by Michael Anderson and starred Rock Hudson, Darren McGavin, Jon Finch, and Bernadette Peters, among others. The miniseries is set in the future and follows the story of humanity's exploration and colonisation of Mars. It portrays a dystopian future where Earth has become overpopulated and devastated by war, leading humans to look to Mars as a new home.

The series is divided into three parts, each focusing on a different period of time. The Martian Chronicles miniseries received mixed reviews upon its release. While some praised the faithful adaptation of the source material and the performances of the cast, others criticised its low production values and uneven storytelling. Some fans of the original book also felt that the miniseries did not capture the depth and scope of Bradbury's work. Ray Bradbury himself called the miniseries 'boring' after he watched it.

Subotsky (shrewdly) bought some Stephen King stories in the early eighties and had a co-producing credit on some of the King stories that were later made by the producer Dino De Laurentiis. Dino De Laurentiis (who died in 2010) was a larger than life cigar chomping Italian film producer who had a remarkably long and eclectic career. He helped to rebuild the shattered Italian film industry after the war but eventually became frustrated by restrictions placed on him there. The law stressed that productions should celebrate the national character and must be made by a majority Italian crew and the squeeze on finances was another notable minus for a producer who was never known for his restraint.

De Laurentiis eventually pitched up in Hollywood where he became famous for his gambling nature, always willing to go for broke on some big project that no one else would touch with a barge pole. An adaption of Frank Herbert's mammoth Dune, Biblical epics, the fantastic grand high camp of Flash Gordon and, perhaps most famously, his 1976 remake of King Kong where his hugely expensive mechanical ape was so rubbish it only appeared in the film for about five seconds. De Laurentiis was an old-fashioned hands-on producer from the Cubby Broccoli/Irving Thalberg school, always full of energy and ideas and determined to make things happen. When the Hannibal script was behind schedule De Laurentiis sent his personal pasta chef to cook for Thomas Harris (!) and he also developed a close friendship with the writer Stephen King in order to produce adaptions of his work.

Milton Subotsky always planned some (mostly aborted) anthology films based on King's stories and one that did get made was 1985's Cat's Eye. Subotsky had a credit on the film. Cat's Eye was directed by Lewis Teague. The film contains three segments - each about half an hour long - that are all connected by a stray cat who plays a role in the stories themselves and has various adventures on the road as the cheesy and oddly stirring eighties score jangles away in jaunty fashion.

The first story on offer in Cat's Eye is called Quitters Inc. Dick Morrison (James Woods) is given the name of a company called Quitters Inc which he is told will cure his obstinate nicotine addiction and decides to check them out. In their swanky city offices he meets the head of the scheme Dr Vinny Donatti (Alan King) - who tells Morrison of their excellent success rates. Morrison enrols in the programme but soon discovers the alarming reason why this unconventional company has such a high success rate. There will be dire consequences for any lapse and these will involve Morrison's family. Quitters Inc let it be known that they will be watching Morrison all the time wherever he is to make sure that he doesn't weaken and smoke.

This is a tense, gripping and fun opening segment to Cat's Eye and probably the strongest story the anthology has to offer. There's a sequence involving a cat that I didn't particularly like watching but James Woods is excellent value as the smirking, twitchy and increasingly stressed out Morrison as he desperately craves a sneaky smoke but is hopelessly paranoid that someone from Quitters Inc is watching him at all times. There is some great stuff in this segment I think. Woods creeping downstairs in the dead of night to look for cigarettes in the drawer but becoming spooked when he suspects someone might be in the house secretly watching him. Another great moment occurs when he weighs up the chances of smoking surreptitiously while stuck in a traffic jam on the motorway with each car around him suddenly seeming disconcertingly suspicious. Alan King is excellent in Quitters Inc too and there is a nice ironic hallucination sequence at a party that uses a cheesy cover of the song Every Breath You Take.

The second story in Cat's Eye is called The Ledge. Norris (Robert Hays) is a washed-up tennis player who plans to elope with the wife of wealthy and compulsive Atlantic City gambler Cressner (Kenneth McMillan). Cressner finds out though and forcibly brings Norris to his high rise apartment where he offers him a wager. If Norris can successfully navigate his way around the outside of the apartment on the small ledge without falling he'll let him go free and he can have Cressner's wife and a lump sum of money to boot. Cressner is an enjoyably horrible sleazebag who plants heroin in the car of Norris to assure he complies with the little game he has devised.

This is another segment that is surprisingly gripping and taut. Interestingly, Cat's Eye eschews gore and traditional horror for a darkly comic Twilight Zone ambiance. Robert Hays - best known for his turn in Airplane - is very good here in a straight role and Kenneth McMillan has a lot of fun as the sleazy Cressner, laughing as Norris wobbles and clings around the ledge with the wind whistling around him, always a moment away from falling to his death. The attempt by Norris to painstakingly get around the outside of the building on this tiny ledge is nicely staged with a good deal of tension and acrophobics everywhere will certainly find this a tense experience. Things turn out pretty much as you expect they will but The Ledge is not bad at all and gleans some dark comic value from an annoying pigeon that dogs Hays as he nervously works his way around the apartment.

The final story in the anthology is called The General and features the cat that has appeared throughout the film to the frequent strains of a cover version of Every Breath You Take. The cat's wandering minstrel adventures seem to have a happy ending when he is taken in by a little girl called Amanda (Drew Barrymore) who names him "General". Things get slightly bizarre with this segment though for the premise is that a little miniature troll/goblin sneaks out of a hole in Amanda's room each night and attempts to steal her breath - in addition to menacing the parrot and generally causing a mess.

Naturally, Amanda's parents blame the cat for all this kerfuffle and plan to be rid of him. Can General somehow save Amanda and himself with a well placed paw or two in the mug of this shadowy and diminutive gremlin? This is a fairly strange end to Cat's Eye with some slightly dated eighties special effects but the little troll creature - created by Carlo Rambaldi - is quite good fun (he even has his own sword!) and although this story is frankly ridiculous it is oddly watchable because you do find yourself rooting for the cat to dispense some moggy justice and save little Drew Barrymore.

On the whole, Cat's Eye is actually quite good with an enjoyably dated eighties soundtrack and score, a sense of irony, some black humour and plenty of Stephen King in-jokes. "Who writes this crap?" mutters Woods watching The Dead Zone on television - in addition to some nods to Cujo, Christine and Pet Semetary. If you had to have a quibble you could probably say Cat's Eye lacked sufficient twists. James Woods and Alan King are both terrific though in Quitters Inc and Hays and McMillan are not far behind for The Ledge. The first two stories were taken from King's Night Shift short story collection and are both very entertaining. The General - which was written for the film - is not as strong but gains a certain charm from its pure weirdness. This is a strange anthology, more Twilight Zone than Amicus, but not bad at all with two decent segments and an interesting cast.

Milton Subotsky then co-produced (and even had a cameo) the 1986 film Maximum Overdrive, an adaptation of Stephen King's story Trucks. King directed the film himself and later admitted he was so "coked out" that he had no idea what he was doing or where he was. The film is about vehicles and machines coming to life and running down humans. Trust me when I say this all plays out on the screen a lot less entertainingly than that plot synopsis sounds on paper. Maximum Overdrive was panned by the critics and bombed at the box-office.

Subotsky then co-produced Sometimes They Come Back, a television film based on the story by Stephen King. Sometimes They Come Back was directed by Tom McLoughlin. Jim

Norman (Tim Matheson) returns to his home town to take a teaching position. The town has painful memories though and he'd rather not be here. When he was a child his brother Wayne (Chris Demetral) was killed in a tunnel where some teenage greaser hooligans were trying to rob him. The greasers all died too when a train hit their car. Jim was the only survivor from the incident. As Jim settles into his teaching position back in his home town, there are a spate of deaths involving the students which appear to be suicides. However the students are replaced one by one by students who look just like the greasers from the tunnel incident all those years ago. Can it be true that they have returned from the grave to extract revenge on Jim?

Sometimes They Come Back is a decent enough Stephen King adaptation and certainly stronger than some of the more forgettable miniseries and tv shows based on the author's work. It's a million times better than, for example, the dismal and best forgotten attempts to turn Under the Dome and The Mist into television shows. Interestingly, this story was apparently going to be one of the segments in the 1985 anthology film Cat's Eye but became a full length film instead. I'm not sure if this was originally planned to be a theatrical feature but one would presume that was the case with Dino De Laurentiis producing.

The familiar staples of Stephen King filter through the story. A small town where a teacher/writer is haunted by the past etc. Although the premise sounds quite grim this is not one of the bleakest King adaptations and seeks to give you a happy ending of sorts. It might be a trifle sentimental for some in the end but I didn't mind. Tim Matheson is likeable enough as the troubled hero and it's nice to see Brooke Adams (a genre favourite through films like Invasion of the Body Snatchers and The Dead Zone) here too as his wife.

The film is a little on the slow side but the flashbacks are generally well done. There is a distinct lack of gore and blood for those who like that sort of thing although you do get a few zombie type effects. The direction is competent without threatening to be much more than that but the story always manages to keep our attention and the cast all play the premise well. This particular Stephen King adaptation has been a little forgotten over the years but it's certainly not bad at all and perhaps even a little underrated. If you found the original story interesting and have never seen the film then you may well enjoy this.

One of the last contributions of Subotsky to the film industry was a co-producer role in the largely forgotten Pierce Brosnan film The Lawnmower Man (a film which had little to do with the Stephen King story on which it was based). Sadly, 1991 would mark the last time that Milton made any contributions to the film industry. Milton Subotsky died of heart disease in 1991, at the age of 69. He left behind a rich legacy of horror and fantasy still being discovered and enjoyed by new generations. "Rosenberg, who was the money man, was always in America and we never met him," said Ingrid Pitt. "But Milton was an angel. He was often on set and he had a way of making you feel wanted. We used to sit around and talk about medicine. He always thought he had something wrong with him."

Max Rosenberg helped produce several films after Amicus wound up although he was often uncredited. Some of these films have been largely forgotten and he was associated with a few stinkers (1988's Invasion Earth: The Aliens Are Here is probably one of the worst films ever made AND padded out with clips from classic sci-fi films to bump it up feature length). Not all of Rosenberg's non-Amicus efforts have been forgotten though. Far from it. We should remember that Rosenberg and Subotsky produced a film adaptation of Harold Pinter's The Birthday Party in 1968 for Palomar Pictures. This was only the second film directed by William Friedkin. Friedkin would direct The French Connection and The Exorcist in the next five years. Rosenberg had been called in as a 'line producer' to get the film made.

This adaptation of Pinter's 'comedy of menace' features Robert Shaw as Stanley. Stanley is a man staying in what appears to be a run down boarding house run by an old couple. Two men arrive and begin to badger Stanley with questions that frequently don't make much sense. The story is, like Pinter's work in general, open to interpretation, but perhaps mostly about free will. It's a surreal play and the dialogue is amusingly bizarre and often based on the trivial and mundane. "Have you had your cornflakes? Were they nice?"

The wonderful Dandy Nichols plays the old lady Meg and you couldn't think of anyone better to dispense the Pinter lines for the character. "What are reading?" she asks her husband Petey (Moultrie Kelsall) when he's clearly reading the newspaper. "Is it good?" Anyone familiar with The Birthday Party will find the mere mention of cornflakes and fried bread funny. Best of all though in the film is that we get Patrick Magee as McCann - one of the two mysterious men who arrive to drive Stanley bonkers. This is quite a conventional performance by Magee's standards but he's terrific throughout the film. The Birthday Party is a very interesting and well directed adaptation of this famous play and worth watching.

The first film that Rosenberg produced after Amicus wound up was 1977's The Incredible Melting Man. The start of the film proudly announces this is a Rosenberg/Gelfman production (Gelfman is Samuel W Gelfman). The Incredible Melting Man is something of a cult film today although only because it is a famously bad one. The film was written and directed by William Sachs. The plot has astronauts encountering a deadly burst of radiation while on a space mission to Saturn. Colonel Steve West (Alex Rebar) is the only survivor but on his return to Earth he wakes up in a hospital to discover that something most alarming has happened as a consequence of the radiation. West seems to be slowly melting! He's soon on the run and completely insane, murdering whoever he runs into.

Here's the strange thing about The Incredible Melting Man. Sachs wrote and directed the film as a spoof of old sci-fi horror films. It was supposed to be a comedy. However, Rosenberg and Gelfman felt that a 'straight' horror film would be more lucrative so they basically changed the film from a comic one into a horror film and inserted several new hastily filmed scenes - all of this done without Sachs, who later predictably complained that his original intent had been ruined. So, as a consequence, The Incredible Melting Man is a bizarre mix of the silly and the horrific. You have Rick Baker's enjoyably disgusting melting man effects and several 'horror' moments like a head floating in a river but you also get lashings of Ed Wood style ineptitude and some of the worst acting you've ever seen in your life. The Incredible Melting Man is though, for better or for worse, an experience if nothing else.

In 1982, Rosenberg had an uncredited producing role on Paul Schrader's interesting (if not entirely successful) 'reimagining' of Cat People. The year before he had a similar role on the 'killer kids' horror film Bloody Birthday. Bloody Birthday is an exploitation film about three evil little kids born during a solar eclipse who set about murdering literally everyone - including their teacher! The most amazing thing about Bloody Birthday is that they somehow got José Ferrer to make an appearance! Rosenberg's last credits as a producer included the television movie Anything to Survive in 1990, and another television film called Survive the Savage Sea in 1992. Both of these films were 'survival' stories, featuring Alaska and the high seas respectively.

Rosenberg's last film was Perdita Durango (aka Dance with the Devil), a 1997 action/horror film directed by Álex de la Iglesia and based on Barry Gifford's novel 59° and Raining: The Story of Perdita Durango. The film had a strong cast with Rosie Perez, Javier Bardem, and James Gandolfini but this eccentric and violent picture met with mixed reviews. Max Rosenberg died in Los Angeles, California in 2004, at the age of 89. Even near the end of his life, Rosenberg was still putting in a full day's work in his office and planning new projects. Rosenberg was responsible for fifty films being produced and along with Milton Subotsky made a fantastic contribution to British horror film history.

In 2006, the film producer Robert Katz resurrected the Amicus name. Katz had known Max Rosenberg and acquired the Amicus rights from Rosenberg's estate. The 2007 Stuart Gordon film Stuck, which got good reviews, was released as an Amicus film. But it wasn't really an Amicus film was it? Stuck is a very American Hollywood film made in 2007. It has absolutely nothing to do with the Amicus we know and love at all. Katz apparently had plans to remake The House That Dripped blood and Dr Terror's House of Horrors but thankfully this never transpired. Doubtless the remakes would have been transplanted to America and had rap music intros or something.

In more recent years, the independent Fife based Hex Studios have announced plans to resurrect Amicus and make an anthology film. Hex apparently got the rights from Milton Subotsky's family. I'm happy for Hex (who I'm sure are nice people and I don't doubt they love and respect the Amicus films) to make an anthology horror film and good luck to them with that but I'm less happy at the thought of this film being branded an Amicus film. We should probably leave Amicus in the 1960s and 1970s and enjoy those films for what they now are - highly entertaining period pieces. The Amicus films may have been cost effective but they had serious talent both behind and in front of the camera. It is almost impossible to replicate those enviable conditions today.

A while back now, I found an old article which was about the history of Amicus Productions. The article could barely contain its snooty disdain for the Amicus films, more or less dismissing them as cheaply made rubbish. Milton Subotsky was largely portrayed in the article as a hack who stole a living churning out these daft films. The article also seemed to think the sci-fi western Welcome to Blood City was an Amicus film and that Amicus films were never camp like the Hammer films - despite the fact that things like Vault of Horror and The Beast Must Die could outcamp most of the Hammer catalogue with one arm tied behind their back.

I suppose the point I'm making is that Milton Subotsky and Max Rosenberg never quite seem to get the credit they deserve. They made a raft of films that I still enjoy watching year after year. Both of these men deserve their own cloud in British horror film heaven if you ask me. The history of British horror films just wouldn't have been the same without them and not nearly as much fun. It's a shame that Amicus didn't last a little longer but we'll always have the films to entertain us. What better way is there to celebrate Halloween than dimming the lights, drawing the curtains, and digging out an Amicus anthology film?